James Tissot

Life of our Saviour Jesus Christ

three hundred and sixty-five compositions from the four gospels; Volume 1

James Tissot

Life of our Saviour Jesus Christ
three hundred and sixty-five compositions from the four gospels; Volume 1
ISBN/EAN: 9783741116827

Manufactured in Europe, USA, Canada, Australia, Japa

Cover: Foto ©Angelika Wolter / pixelio.de

Manufactured and distributed by brebook publishing software (www.brebook.com)

James Tissot

Life of our Saviour Jesus Christ

THE LIFE

OF

OUR LORD JESUS CHRIST

VOL. I

THE ADORATION OF THE MAGI

THE LIFE OF OUR SAVIOUR

JESVS CHRIST

THREE HUNDRED AND SIXTY-FIVE COMPOSITIONS
FROM THE FOUR GOSPELS
WITH NOTES AND EXPLANATORY DRAWINGS

BY

J. JAMES TISSOT

Notes translated by Mrs ARTHUR BELL (N. d'Anvers)

VOL. I.

EN ipse stat post parietem nostrum, respiciens per fenestras, prospiciens per cancellos.

(*Cant.*, II, 9.)

BEHOLD, he standeth behind our wall, he looketh forth at the windows shewing himself through the lattice.

(*Solom..Song.* II, 9.)

NEW YORK
THE McCLURE-TISSOT COMPANY
MDCCCXCIX

Copyright 1895 by J. James Tissot.
Copyright 1896 by J. James Tissot.
Copyright 1899 by J. James Tissot.

All illustrations entered according to the act of Congress, in the years 1895, 1896 and 1899, by J. James Tissot, in the Office of the Librarian of Congress, at Washington.

C'est à vous, Monsieur Gladstone, auquel votre pays a décerné de son vivant le titre de grand homme, que je dédie cette traduction de mon livre.

Je vous remercie du grand honneur que vous avez fait à mon œuvre en acceptant cette dédicace.

J. James Tissot

15 octobre 1897
abbaye de Buillon

THE LIFE OF OUR LORD JESUS CHRIST

INTRODUCTION

INTRODUCTION

N my return from Jerusalem, in March 1887, I went to see my father, a Christian of the old-fashioned sort, and a devout Catholic. I shewed him my sketches, drawings, and all the documents I had brought back with me from beyond the sea. When he saw the various scenes in their exact proportions, the view of Golgotha especially, he exclaimed : « It seems I have got to change all my preconceived ideas about things! What! Is not Calvary after all a lofty sugar-loaf mountain, covered with rocks and brushwood? »
« Well, no », I replied, « Calvary, though it did occupy the summit of the town, was not more than from 20 to 22 feet high at the most. In just the same way the Holy Sepulchre was near it, but under conditions totally different from what you imagine. Your error is very much that of most of the faithful. For a long time the imagination of the Christian world has been led astray by the fancies of artists; there is a whole army of delusions to be overturned, before any ideas can be entertained approaching the truth in the slightest degree. All the schools of art have worked, more or less conscientiously, to lead astray public opinion in these matters. Some of these schools, preoccupied, as were those of the Renaissance, with the setting of the scenes represented, others, like those of the mystics, with the inner meaning of the various events, were of one accord in ignoring the evidence of history, and dispensing with topographical accuracy. Is it not time in this exact century, when such words as nearly or almost have no longer any value, to restore to reality — I do not say to realism — the rights which have been filched from it? »

This is why, attracted as I was by the divine figure of Jesus and the touching scenes recorded in the Gospels, I determined to go to Palestine on a pilgrimage of exploration, hoping to restore to those scenes as far as possible the actual aspect assumed by them when they occurred. For this, was it not indeed absolutely necessary to study on the spot, the configuration of the landscape, and the character of the inhabitants, endeavouring to trace back from their modern representatives through successive generations the original types of the races of Palestine, and the various constituents which go to make up what is called antiquity?

I started on October 15th 1886. I was then just fifty years old.

Arrived in Egypt, I recognized immediately that I had no disillusioning to dread there. Alexandria and Cairo alone were enough to recompense me for my journey, for they impressed me at once with a sense of their antiquity. With such data before me, it seemed almost unnecessary to go further, for here the past was palpable in the actual present, and it appeared to me easy enough to remove the thin layer of modernism encrusting it, so as to bring to light without delay the vestiges of olden times. When I got to Palestine, however, my impressions were different; I felt that Africa is not the whole of the Orient, that there, race, customs, materials of the towns, and yet more the landscapes, the structure of the soil, were all dissimilar to those of the Holy Land. Then, when I went further north to Nazareth, to Lebanon, to Damascus, I felt the presence of the Turkish race, that is to say, of men from the more northerly Turkey, who bring with them their manners, their sensuality, their peculiar costumes, such as their robes lined with fur and loaded with embroidery, requiring quite special adjustment. I was then able, by a comparison between the north and the south to evolve for myself a more complete, and at the same time, a more precise idea of the Land of Judæa. I recognized, for instance, in the Jewish costume the use of the sash, required by law, which ordered the separation of the pure from the impure ; and also the use of that piece of material of the form of a scarf with four corners, which the Jews always wear over their other garments, each corner bearing the four letters of the Jewish name for Jehovah, J. H. V. H. — With the women, the hair was completely covered and their draperies disguised the form of the body as much as possible, in obedience to that same refinement of modesty which led to the regulation of the height of the steps leading up to the Temple.

With regard to the general character of the buildings, the differences were equally striking. In Africa and the North of Palestine, where wood is employed, the design and decorations alike of private houses and public edifices are quite unlike those of Judæa, where wood is not to be had, and where it never was to be had, for we know that that used in the construction of the palaces and of the porches of the Temple was brought from Lebanon. Every house had a dome surmounting the roof, and this dome could be very distinctly seen, the numerous groups of rounded roofs contrasting very forcibly with the flat ones of Northern and Southern towns.

These general data put me on the right tack for the studies I had to pursue. *All that was now needed was intuition.* Every work, no matter what, has its own ideal; and the ideal of mine was truth, the truth of the life of Christ. To reproduce with fidelity the divine personality of Jesus, to make Him live again before the eyes of the spectators, to call up the very spirit which shone through His every act, and through all His noble teaching; what could be more fascinating, and at the same time more difficult ? I had to identify myself as much as possible with the Gospels; to read them over and over again a hundred times, and there is no doubt that it is in the Holy Land itself, on the very spots where all the sublime scenes described took place, that the mind is best attuned alike to receive and grasp the significance of every impression. Sometimes, indeed, as I trod the very path over which the feet of the Saviour had passed; when I realized that my eyes were reflecting the very landscape on which He had gazed, I felt that a certain receptivity was induced in my mind which so intensified my powers of intuition, that the scenes of the past rose up before my mental vision in a peculiar and striking manner. In the same way, penetrated as I became with the spirit of the race to which the actors in these scenes belonged, realizing as I did, the character of the districts in which they lived and moved; with the local colour of the familiar objects by which they were surrounded; when, thus prepared, I meditated on any special incident in its own particular sanctuary, and was thus brought into touch with the actual setting of every scene, the facts I was anxious to evoke were revealed to me in all their ideality and under the most striking forms. Is not the artist, indeed, a kind of sensitive plant, the activity of which, when concentrated on a certain point, is intensified, and through a kind of hyperæsthesia, is powerfully affected by contact with objects outside of itself;

this contact producing vivid images on the brain? — I will not enter here into the details of the brilliant light, almost amounting to divination, which was thrown on various points by the sight of certain stones, and certain apparently insignificant topographical details; to do so would be to risk being accused of mysticism. I realized fully that what I still needed to complete the necessary education for my task was quiet meditation. Indispensable as this is to every one who contemplates an important work, is it not especially needed when what is in prospect is a journey to the Holy Land, where every plot of ground is a sanctuary? I did my very utmost, therefore, to secure for myself this final preparation.

The Gospels, having never yet been treated in the graphic manner proposed by me, I had found — all important point for an artist — altogether untrodden ground, where I need have no fear of plagiarism. The remembrance of the works of other masters hampered me not at all, for I did not see as they had done. What I sought, I repeat once more, was to have my emotions acted on directly by the life of Our Lord, by traversing the same districts as He did, by gazing upon the same landscapes, and by hunting out the traces of the civilization, which prevailed during His lifetime. The outcome of all this is a series of pictures, the result of vivid and sincerely rendered impressions, which I now present to the public. I must add that, in addition to authorized authorities, I have consulted a vast number of valuable manuscripts. Amongst the ancients: Josephus, the Talmud, the Apocryphal Gospels, the earliest Christian authors; amongst the moderns: Von Munk, D'Sepp, Stapfer, P. Didon and P. Ollivier, have helped me greatly. The plan in relief of the Temple of Herod, so conscientiously executed by the German Architect, Herr Schieck, served as the basis of my reconstitution of the same building. I also consulted Catherine Emmerich, whose visions, generally so precise, impressed me greatly.

Now that my meditations have taken tangible form, and after ten years of work this new life of Our Saviour Jesus Christ is about to appear, bearing the precise character of things actually seen and experienced, I must just add: I do not pretend to assert that the events I recall happened exactly as I relate them; far from that. I have only endeavoured to supply a personal interpretation based on serious data, and intended to remove as far as possible vague and uncertain impressions. I have thus, I hope, accomplished a useful work, I have taken one step in the direction of the truth, and set up one landmark which will point the way to be followed for penetrating yet further into this inexhaustible subject. If some other in his turn wishes to study and elucidate it yet further, let him make haste; for the data still existing, the documents of past centuries still surviving, will, doubtless, ere long, in these days of the invasion of the engineer and the railway, disappear before the irresistible impulse of the aggressive modern spirit.

James TISSOT.

DIVISION OF THE WORK

THE HOLY CHILDHOOD

THE MINISTRY

THE HOLY WEEK

THE PASSION

THE RESURRECTION

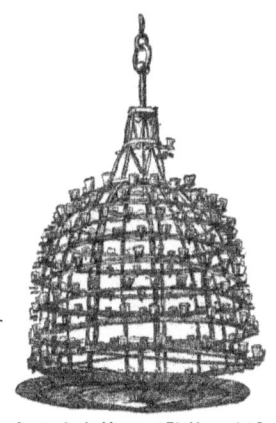

Lamps in the Mosque of El-Aksa.   J.-J. T

All illustrations entered according to act of Congress, in the years 1895 and 1896, by J.-J. Tissot
in the Office of the Librarian of Congress, at Washington.

THE HOLY CHILDHOOD

Corinthian Capital.

THE HOLY CHILDHOOD

Vision of Zacharias
Saint Luke — Chap. 1

ACTUM est autem, quum sacerdotio fungeretur in ordine vicis suæ ante Deum,

9. Secundum consuetudinem sacerdotii, sorte exiit ut incensum poneret, ingressus in templum Domini.

10. Et omnis multitudo populi erat orans foris hora incensi.

11. Apparuit autem illi angelus Domini, stans a dextris altaris incensi.

12. Et Zacharias turbatus est videns, et timor irruit super eum.

13. Ait autem ad illum angelus : Ne timeas, Zacharia, quoniam exaudita est deprecatio tua, et uxor tua Elisabeth pariet tibi filium, et vocabis nomen ejus Joannem.

ND it came to pass, that while he executed the priest's office before God in the order of his course,

9. According to the custom of the priest's office, his lot was to burn incense when he went into the temple of the Lord.

10. And the whole multitude of the people were praying without at the time of incense.

11. And there appeared unto him an angel of the Lord standing on the right side of the altar of incense.

12. And when Zacharias saw him, he was troubled, and fear fell upon him.

13. But the angel said unto him, Fear not, Zacharias : for thy prayer is heard ; and thy wife Elisabeth shall bear thee a son, and thou shalt call his name John.

14. Et erit gaudium tibi, et exsultatio, et multi in nativitate ejus gaudebunt.

15. Erit enim magnus coram Domino; et vinum et siceram non bibet, et Spiritu sancto replebitur adhuc ex utero matris suæ.

16. Et multos filiorum Israel convertet ad Dominum Deum ipsorum.

17. Et ipse præcedet ante illum in spiritu et virtute Eliæ, ut convertat corda patrum in filios et incredulos ad prudentiam justorum, parare Domino plebem perfectam.

18. Et dixit Zacharias ad angelum: Unde hoc sciam? ego enim sum senex, et uxor mea processit in diebus suis.

19. Et respondens angelus dixit ei: Ego sum Gabriel, qui adsto ante Deum; et missus sum loqui ad te, et hæc tibi evangelizare.

20. Et ecce eris tacens, et non poteris loqui, usque in diem quo hæc fiant, pro eo quod non credidisti verbis meis quæ implebuntur in tempore suo.

21. Et erat plebs exspectans Zachariam, et mirabantur quod tardaret ipse in templo.

22. Egressus autem non poterat loqui ad illos, et cognoverunt quod visionem vidisset in templo. Et ipse erat innuens illis, et permansit mutus.

14. And thou shalt have joy and gladness; and many shall rejoice at his birth.

15. For he shall be great in the sight of the Lord, and shall drink neither wine nor strong drink; and he shall be filled with the Holy Ghost, even from his mother's womb.

16. And many of the children of Israel shall he turn to the Lord their God.

17. And he shall go before him in the spirit and power of Elias, to turn the hearts of the fathers to the children, and the disobedient to the wisdom of the just, to make ready a people prepared for the Lord.

18. And Zacharias said unto the angel, Whereby shall I know this? for I am an old man, and my wife well stricken in years.

19. And the angel answering said unto him, I am Gabriel, that stand in the presence of God; and am sent to speak unto thee, and to shew thee these glad tidings.

20. And, behold, thou shalt be dumb, and not able to speak, until the day that these things shall be performed, because thou believedst not my words, which shall be fulfilled in their season.

21. And the people waited for Zacharias, and marvelled that he tarried so long in the temple.

22. And when he came out, he could not speak unto them; and they perceived that he had seen a vision in the temple. For he beckoned unto them, and remained speechless.

We know that the Temple was situated on the plateau of Mount Moriah, of which it occupied but a very small portion. All around it were grouped the various courts for the Priests and the worshippers, male and female, whilst these courts were surrounded, in

their turn, by the so-called Chel, a kind of narrow rampart to which Gentiles were not admitted.

Another and larger enclosure, intended for the general public, bore the name of the Court of the Gentiles; beyond which the esplanade extended to the Cloisters, which entirely surrounded it; on the south, the Royal Cloister, with four rows of columns; on the east, the Porch of Solomon, including two rows of columns only; on the west and north, simple cloisters, less frequented than the others, because they were too much exposed to the heat of the sun.

Fountain of the Virgin at Aïn-Karim. J.-J T.

The Temple properly so called was divided into three parts : the vestibule, called the Olam, the Holy Place, called the Hekal, and the Holy of Holies, entered by the High Priest only. The Hekal was separated from the Holy of Holies by a double curtain, between the two portions of which a space was left wide enough for a low wall one cubit high, which extended right across. In front of this curtain which Saint Mark designates by the Greek word « Catapetasma », and which Josephus asserts he saw at Rome amongst the spoils of the Temple, still all stained with the blood from the daily sprinklings, was the Altar of sweet-smelling incense. It was a small table of shittim wood, which is a kind of acacia, covered with thin plates of gold, and one cubit wide by two high. At each of the four corners rose a pointed horn, and it was surrounded by a floral ornamentation, forming a kind of crown. Incense was offered up twice every day, in the morning and the evening by the Priest on whom the lot fell for the performance of this service. This incense was prepared in a peculiar manner : seven different plants were used, and one of these plants, known to the Abtinos family, whose business it was to make the incense, had the property, when burnt, of rising in an upright column of smoke, instead of dispersing in clouds on issuing from the censer. The Priest on duty brought the censer, a vessel made of fine Pernaim gold, with a long handle, into the Hekal and, having first put fire in it, taken from the Altar of Burnt Offerings, he added the incense, placed the sacred vessel containing it on the Altar and withdrew from the Holy Place. The smoke which rose up from the burning incense was very thick and escaped in masses through the little windows overlooking the vestibule, above the door adorned with a golden vine and thence made its way through the upper part of the entrance to the Olam, the lower portion of which was closed by the curtain from Babylon, embroidered with flowers, referred to by Josephus. Sometimes, when the wind blew from the West, the scent of the incense burning in the Temple was perceptible some six leagues off, on the borders of the Dead Sea and Jericho. Rabbi Eleazer ben Doly relates that the goats on his father's property on the Ackuras Mountains used to sneeze when they smelt the incense.

At the time of Herod, the Ark was no longer in the Temple, but a stone was preserved there which was said to have upheld it and to which the name of the « Schetiyah » was given. It rose to a height of about three finger-lengths from the ground, and ceremonial usage required that the High Priest should place the censer of incense upon it, on the Day of Atonement. Tradition relates that this stone was the first work of God here below, and that from it the earth issued forth and spread towards the four points of the compass : this is why the Schetiyah is called the Foundation Stone.

Here are a few details as to the costume of the Priest. He wore a robe of white linen, woven in such a manner that a pattern like that of a chess-board was formed in the material. This robe was kept in place by bands fastened to the shoulders, and the sleeves were arranged so that they escaped being stained with the blood of the victims constantly handled by their wearers.

The Vision of Zacharias

The Levite wore a particular kind of sash, made of very light stuff, wrinkled like the skin of a snake. It was adorned from end to end with purple, azure-blue and scarlet embroideries, and was about four finger-lengths wide by thirty-five cubits long. To dispose of a sash so long, it had to be wound round and round a very great number of times. To begin with, it was passed three times round the upper part of the chest, then a great bow was made, the two divisions of which fell down in front to the thighs; then the sash was wound round three times more, rather lower down than before, and a second bow was made with drooping loops. Yet again the sash was wound round, this time till it reached the hips. Even now there still remained two long ends, and, to prevent them from dropping on the ground, they were passed through the nine bands round the body and carried up to the shoulders, where they were fastened, and from which they drooped, more or less according to the figure of the wearer.

The Priests had to walk barefoot on the cedar floor of the Hekal and on the flagstones of the Court of the Priests. Various maladies resulted from this rule, and it was the special duty of a doctor, who lived in the El Moked, or chamber adjoining the Court of the Priests, to cure these ailments. The name has been preserved of a certain Rabbi ben Ahai, who was said to be very skilful in effecting cures. He subjected his patients to a particular diet, forbidding them to drink water when they ate meat, and prescribing a different wine to be taken with each article of food.

In this same El Moked, a fire was kept up, at which old men were allowed to warm themselves. It is even said that beneath the two courts just mentioned, and behind the rooms where the musicians kept their instruments, a kind of heating apparatus was arranged, consisting of pipes running beneath the flagstones, through which passed the hot air from the pavilion.

Beneath the Priests' Court there was a passage through which could pass any of those who, in their nocturnal vigil, had contracted any impurity. All these details are given in the Talmuds.

The Testing of the Suitors of the Virgin

The Testing of the Suitors of the Virgin

According to the Apocryphal Gospels, the claims of the various suitors of the Holy Virgin were tested in the following manner. The suitors, who had all to be of the race of David, and must none of them have contracted any other alliance, each brought with him a rod. All these rods were placed in the Holy of Holies, and the owner of the rod which should flower would be the one chosen to be the husband of Mary. The legend tells us that there were three thousand suitors, but that Joseph, dreading the test, held himself aloof on the appointed day; however, the High Priest, Abiathar, wearing the sacerdotal robes with the twelve bells, came forth from the Holy of Holies, bearing in his hand the rod of Joseph, which had been pointed out to him by an angel. When it was given to Joseph, a white dove issued from it and, soaring up to Heaven, disappeared.

When the High Priest had to enter the Holy of Holies, a long cord was fastened round his waist, the end of which trailed far behind him and remained outside in the Hekal, whilst the wearer, drawing aside in succession the various curtains, passed beyond them and disappeared. If the tinkling of the twelve bells at the edge of his robe ceased for too long at a time, the watchers concluded that death had overtaken him, and as no one was allowed to enter the Holy of Holies under any pretext whatever, the body was drawn out by means of the cord.

Betrothal of the Holy Virgin and St. Joseph
Saint Luke — Chap. 1

 N mense autem sexto, missus est angelus Gabriel a Deo in civitatem Galilææ, cui nomen Nazareth,

27. Ad virginem desponsatam viro, cui nomen erat Joseph, de domo David, et nomen virginis Maria.

Jewish weddings were celebrated on the fourth day of the week, or the fifth if the bride were a widow. It must, therefore, have been on a Wednesday or a Thursday, that the marriage of Joseph and Mary took place. The bride always entered her new home at sunset. This part of the ceremony was looked upon as most important; and the marriage itself was also sometimes spoken of as the Reception or Introduction of the wife. The bride and bridegroom often each

 ND in the sixth month the angel Gabriel was sent from God unto a city of Galilee, named Nazareth,

27. To a virgin espoused to a man whose name was Joseph, of the house of David, and the virgin's name was Mary.

wore a crown. They advanced to the sound of a drum and other instruments of music, beneath a canopy of painted material, from which, in the case of wealthy families, ornaments of gold were suspended.

Sometimes the canopy of painted stuff was replaced by a cupola of woven papyrus stems, forming a kind of trellis work, from which all manner of objects hung down. Often, too, the bridal crowns bore plaques of gold, on which were representations of

The Betrothal of the Holy Virgin and St. Joseph.

towns, either engraved or in « repoussé » work, known as Golden Tower ornaments. In other cases the crowns were made of brocade, or some sort of gleaming stuff, or even of petrified materials, adorned with paintings in sulphur, or yet again of petrified olive leaves. All this accumulation of details, which varied slightly at different times, reflects very clearly the manners and customs of this transition period.

The Annunciation
Saint Luke – Chap. 1

t ingressus angelus ad eam dixit : Ave, gratia plena; Dominus tecum ; benedicta tu in mulieribus.

ND the angel came in unto her, and said, Hail, thou that art highly favoured, the Lord is with thee: blessed art thou among women.

29. Quæ quum audisset, turbata est in sermone ejus, et cogitabat qualis esset ista salutatio.

29. And when she saw him, she was troubled at his saying, and cast in her mind what manner of salutation this should be.

30. Et ait angelus ei : Ne timeas, Maria, invenisti enim gratiam apud Deum ;

30. And the angel said unto her : Fear not, Mary, for thou hast found favour with God.

31. Ecce concipies in utero, et paries filium, et vocabis nomen ejus Jesum.

31. And, behold, thou shalt conceive in thy womb, and bring forth a son, and shalt call his name Jesus.

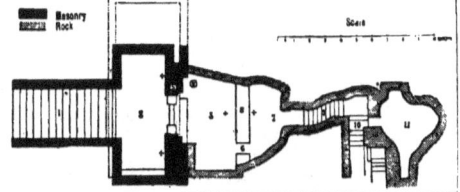

The double pointed lines indicate the actual site of the house.
1 Fifteen steps leading from the Church to the sanctuary.
2 Chapel of the Angel.
3 Chapel of the Annunciation.
4 Broken column.
5 Walled in column.
6 Entrance to the dark chapel.
7 The dark chapel.
8 Altar of the Flight into Egypt.
9 Steps leading up to the Kitchen of the Holy Virgin.
10 Staircase communicating with the Vestry.
11 Kitchen of the Holy Virgin.

32. Hic erit magnus, et Filius Altissimi vocabitur, et dabit illi Dominus Deus sedem David, patris ejus; et regnabit in domo Jacob in æternum.

32. He shall be great, and shall be called the Son of the Highest; and the Lord God shall give unto him the throne of his father David;

33. Et regni ejus non erit finis.

33. And he shall reign over the house of Jacob for ever; and of his kingdom

THE HOLY CHILDHOOD

The Annunciation.

The Holy Virgin as a girl.

34. Dixit autem Maria ad angelum : Quomodo fiet istud, quoniam virum non cognosco?

35. Et respondens angelus dixit ei : Spiritus sanctus superveniet in te, et virtus Altissimi obumbrabit tibi. Ideoque et quod nascetur ex te sanctum, vocabitur Filius Dei.

36. Et ecce Elisabeth, cognata tua, et ipsa concepit filium in senectute sua; et hic mensis sextus est illi, quæ vocatur sterilis ;

37. Quia non erit impossibile apud Deum omne verbum.

there shall be no end.

34. Then said Mary unto the angel : How shall this be, seeing I know not a man?

35. And the angel answered and said unto her : The Holy Ghost shall come upon thee, and the power of the Highest shall overshadow thee : therefore also that holy thing which shall be born of thee shall be called the Son of God.

36. And, behold, thy cousin Elisabeth, she hath also conceived a son in her old age : and this is the sixth month with her, who was called barren.

37. For with God nothing shall be impossible.

38. Dixit autem Maria: Ecce ancilla Domini, fiat mihi secundum verbum tuum. Et discessit ab illa angelus.

38. And Mary said: Behold the handmaid of the Lord; be it unto me according to thy word. And the angel departed from her.

The Visitation
Saint Luke — Chap. 1

XSURGENS autem Maria in diebus illis abiit in montana cum festinatione, in civitatem Juda;
40. Et intravit in domum Zachariæ, et salutavit Elisabeth.
41. Et factum est, ut audivit salutationem Mariæ Elisabeth, exsultavit infans in utero ejus, et repleta est Spiritu sancto Elisabeth.

42. Et exclamavit voce magna, et dixit: Benedicta tu inter mulieres, et benedictus fructus ventris tui.

43. Et unde hoc mihi ut veniat mater Domini mei ad me?

44. Ecce enim ut facta est vox salutationis tuæ in auribus meis, exsultavit in gaudio infans in utero meo.

45. Et beata, quæ credidisti, quoniam perficientur ea, quæ dicta sunt tibi a

ND Mary arose in those days, and went into the hill country with haste, into a city of Juda;
40. And entered into the house of Zacharias, and saluted Elisabeth.
41. And it came to pass, that, when Elisabeth heard the salutation of Mary, the babe leaped in her womb; and Elisabeth was filled with the Holy Ghost.

42. And she spake out with a loud voice, and said: Blessed art thou among women, and blessed is the fruit of thy womb.

43. And whence is this to me, that the mother of my Lord should come to me?

44. For, lo, as soon as the voice of thy salutation sounded in mine ears, the babe leaped in my womb for joy.

45. And blessed is she that believed: for there shall be a performance of

The Visitation.

THE HOLY CHILDHOOD

Domino.

56. Mansit autem Maria cum illa quasi mensibus tribus; et reversa est in domum suam.

57. Elisabeth autem impletum est tempus pariendi, et peperit filium.

58. Et audierunt vicini et cognati ejus, quia magnificavit Dominus misericordiam suam cum illa, et congratulabantur ei.

59. Et factum est in die octavo, venerunt circumcidere puerum, et vocabant eum nomine patris sui Zachariam.

60. Et respondens mater ejus, dixit: Nequaquam, sed vocabitur Joannes.

61. Et dixerunt ad illam: Quia nemo est in cognatione tua, qui vocetur hoc nomine.

62. Innuebant autem patri ejus, quem vellet vocari eum.

those things which were told her from the Lord.

56. And Mary abode with her about three months, and returned to her own house.

57. Now Elisabeth's full time came that she should be delivered, and she brought forth a son.

58. And her neighbours and her cousins heard how the Lord had shewed great mercy upon her, and they rejoiced with her.

59. And it came to pass, that on the eighth day they came to circumcise the child, and they called him Zacharias, after the name of his father.

60. And his mother answered and said: Not so, but he shall be called John.

61. And they said unto her: There is none of thy kindred that is called by this name.

62. And they made signs to his father, how he would have him called.

The Magnificat
Saint Luke – Chap. 1

t ait Maria: Magnificat anima mea Dominum;
47. Et exsultavit spiritus meus in Deo salutari meo.
48. Quia respexit humilitatem ancillæ suæ; ecce enim ex hoc beatam me dicent omnes generationes;

ND Mary said: My soul doth magnify the Lord;
47. And my spirit hath rejoiced in God my Saviour.
48. For he hath regarded the low estate of his handmaiden; for, behold, from henceforth all generations shall call me blessed,

THE MAGNIFICAT

THE MAGNIFICAT

49. Quia fecit mihi magna qui potens est, et sanctum nomen ejus.

50. Et misericordia ejus a progenie in progenies timentibus eum.

51. Fecit potentiam in brachio suo; dispersit superbos mente cordis sui.

52. Deposuit potentes de sede, et exaltavit humiles.

53. Esurientes implevit bonis, et divites dimisit inanes.

54. Suscepit Israel, puerum suum, recordatus misericordiæ suæ,

55. Sicut locutus est ad patres nostros, Abraham et semini ejus in sæcula.

56. Mansit autem Maria cum illa quasi mensibus tribus; et reversa est in domum suam.

49. For he that is mighty hath done to me great things, and holy is his name.

50. And his mercy is on them that fear him from generation to generation.

51. He hath shewed strength with his arm, he hath scattered the proud in the imagination of their hearts.

52. He hath put down the mighty from their seats, and exalted them of low degree.

53. He hath filled the hungry with good things, and the rich he hath sent empty away.

54. He hath holpen his servant Israel, in remembrance of his mercy,

55. As he spake to our fathers, to Abraham, and to his seed for ever.

56. And Mary abode with her about three months, and returned to her own house.

The journey from Nazareth to Aïn-Karim, where Elizabeth dwelt, must have taken about four days, the way having been both steep and rough. The hills of Samaria and Judæa, cutting right across the road thither, and the wild valley, known as the Wady-el-Arimaïch, or that of Robbers, which had to be traversed in going from Samaria to Jerusalem, must have made the journey extremely arduous, especially for the Holy Virgin, in the state she was then in. According to the custom of the country Mary had to ride on an ass, Joseph walking beside her. It is natural to suppose that the two travellers, after halting now and again, at the caravansaries by the way, passed the last night at Jerusalem, where Joseph probably had relations, and that they arrived at Aïn-Karim, three hours' journey beyond that town, early on the next day. — Was it at the first interview with Elizabeth that the Virgin uttered the hymn of the Magnificat? Was it not more likely at the time of the private out-pouring of confidences between the two, which must have taken place later on? It seems to us much more natural that it should have been then; we greatly prefer so to consider it, and we have therefore chosen, as the setting of the scene fraught with such sacred mystery, the secluded garden of Elizabeth. In the midst of an exchange of their strange and wonderful experiences, Mary was suddenly possessed by the Spirit of God, and, in a kind of prophetic ecstasy, she poured forth her joy at her coming maternity, her humble acceptance of the will of the Almighty, her inspired insight into the grandeur of the Divine plan, all these various feelings, merged in her virgin soul, and so pervading

her whole personality, that for the moment her own individual life seemed as it were to be suspended. We must not, therefore, look upon the Magnificat as an outburst of loud triumphant joy, such as, if I may so express it, would be natural to an Italian woman, but as the quiet, reverent, almost whispered expression of a spirit moved to its very depths; a prayer, so intensely earnest as to be scarcely audible, the effect of which was yet further intensified by the dumbness of Zacharias, and the emotion of Elizabeth.

The Anxiety of Saint Joseph
Saint Matthew — Chap. 1

ACOB autem genuit Joseph, virum Mariæ, de qua natus est Jesus, qui vocatur Christus.

17. Omnes itaque generationes ab Abraham usque ad David, generationes quatuordecim; et a David usque ad transmigrationem Babylonis, generationes quatuordecim; et a transmigratione Babylonis usque ad Christum generationes quatuordecim.

AND Jacob begat Joseph the husband of Mary, of whom was born Jesus, who is called Christ.

17. So all the generations from Abraham to David are fourteen generations; and from David until the carrying away into Babylon are fourteen generations; and from the carrying away into Babylon unto Christ are fourteen generations.

The anxiety of Saint Joseph.

18. Christi autem generatio sic erat: Quum esset desponsata mater ejus Maria Joseph, antequam convenirent, inventa

18. Now the birth of Jesus Christ was on this wise: When as his mother Mary was espoused to Joseph, before

THE ANXIETY OF SAINT JOSEPH

est in utero habens de Spiritu sancto.

19. Joseph autem, vir ejus, quum esset justus, et nollet eam traducere, voluit occulte dimittere eam.

they came together, she was found with child of the Holy Ghost.

19. Then Joseph her husband, being a just man, and not willing to make her a publick example, was minded to put her away privily.

In Chap. XVI of the so-called Protevangelium of St. James the Less, in the Collection of the Apocryphal Gospels, we are told that Joseph was struck with stupor, and thought to himself: « *What shall I do with her? And he said: If I hide her sin, I shall be guilty according to the Law of God; and if I accuse her and betray her to the Sons of Israel, I fear that I shall be unjust and deliver the blood of the innocent to the condemnation of death. What shall I do with her? I will leave her secretly.* » *Such were the thoughts which haunted the mind of Joseph and hindered him in his work.* — *To explain the point of view of my picture, I must add that I have imagined the following scene. Joseph is in his workshop, which is on the way leading to the well. It is early morning, when the women go to fetch the water needed for the day, and Joseph's tender affection for her to whom he has recently become betrothed leads him to watch for the moment when she will pass. Certain alarming signs about his young bride, though he had been vaguely conscious of them, had not as yet shaken his confidence in her. But now, as he watches her pass his workshop day by day, these signs of something unusual recur to his memory, his anxiety is aroused and at last the truth is forced on his mind beyond a doubt. He can no longer hope that he has been mistaken, he understands it all now; he can work no more; he abandons the task he had begun, and gives himself up to his painful forebodings.*

Saint Joseph

I have accepted the tradition that Saint Joseph practised the trade of a carpenter or something similar to it. According to some traditions he made the yokes of ploughs and the wood-work of implements of husbandry. Others, founded probably on his sojourn in Egypt, say that he made the trellis-work used, especially in that country, to make partitions between the rooms of houses, to take the place of windows and to ornament balconies. However this may be, there is no doubt that Joseph occupied a very humble position. Though he was of royal lineage, his family had retained none of its ancient splendour, and he himself lived in a quiet secluded way, congenial, doubtless, to the humility and modesty of his character.

How old was he at the time of his betrothal to the Virgin? Traditions are by no means unanimous on this point. The Apocryphal Gospel of the Childhood of Jesus, followed by St. Jerome and some others, make him an old man. But against this must be set the Rabbinical doctrine, which looked upon the union of a young girl with an old man as a kind of profanation. Moreover, Joseph was called upon to be the protector of Mary, and the foster father of Christ during His infancy; this double task was an arduous one: would it not be far more suitably fulfilled by a man in the prime of life, than by one already overtaken by the infirmities of age? In my representation of St. Joseph, I took as a model one of the Yemenites, a race of Arabia Petræa, which, thanks to the autonomy it has been able to maintain in the midst of the manifold influences which have so greatly modified other branches of the Jewish race, has remained to the present time one of the noblest and most characteristic groups of purely Jewish descent.

The Vision of St. Joseph
Saint Matthew — Chap. 1

Æc autem eo cogitante, ecce angelus Domini apparuit in somnis ei, dicens : Joseph, fili David, noli timere accipere Mariam conjugem tuam; quod enim in ea natum est, de Spiritu sancto est.

21. Pariet autem filium, et vocabis nomen ejus Jesum; ipse enim salvum faciet populum suum a peccatis eorum.
22. Hoc autem totum factum est, ut adimpleretur quod dictum est a Domino per prophetam dicentem :
23. Ecce virgo in utero habebit, et pariet filium ; et vocabunt nomen ejus Emmanuel, quod est interpretatum : Nobiscum Deus.
24. Exsurgens autem Joseph a somno, fecit sicut præcepit ei angelus Domini, et accepit conjugem suam.
25. Et non cognoscebat eam donec peperit filium suum primogenitum; et vocavit nomen ejus Jesum.

ut while he thought on these things, behold, the angel of the Lord appeared unto him in a dream, saying : Joseph, thou son of David, fear not to take unto thee Mary thy wife; for that which is conceived in her is of the Holy Ghost.

21. And she shall bring forth a son, and thou shalt call his name Jesus; for he shall save his people from their sins.
22. Now all this was done, that it might be fulfilled which was spoken of the Lord by the prophet, saying :
23. Behold, a virgin shall be with child, and shall bring forth a son, and they shall call his name Emmanuel, which being interpreted is : God with us.
24. Then Joseph being raised from sleep did as the angel of the Lord had bidden him, and took unto him his wife.
25. And knew her not till she had brought forth her firstborn son; and he called his name Jesus.

THE VISION OF SAINT JOSEPH

A certain number of apparitions of angels are recorded in the Bible, and in many cases the sacred text describes the form under which these angels appeared.

Generally, Holy Writ speaks of them as having wings, an attribute of their mission as messengers from on high, and with these wings they cover their bodies, as if to mark the fact that they are pure spirits, released from the burden of the flesh. In other cases the wings are not mentioned, but the apparition always assumes a form which implies more or less directly the rôle the messenger has to play here below.

Ezekiel speaks of cherubs or cherubim. The idea of the cherubs or cherubim was, amongst the Jews, associated with the form of some animal, such as the lion, the bull or the eagle, rather than with that of a man. In some visions all four « beasts » appeared together, and each one of them had six wings, covered with eyes within and without. This was the case in the vision of Saint John the Divine, related in Revelation (Chap. IV, verses 7, 8), when he saw, in the midst of the throne and round about the throne, four beasts, the first like a lion, the second like a calf, the third with the face of a man, and the fourth like a flying eagle, « and they rest not day and night, saying: Holy, holy, holy, Lord God Almighty, which was, and is, and is to come. »

It is worthy of remark that the cherub, especially when it had the face of a man, was provided with three pairs of wings, one pair to veil the face, another to veil the body and the third used in flight. This last detail is not given in the passage of the Apocalypse just quoted, but it is very distinctly indicated elsewhere in the Bible, and this was probably the form adopted by Solomon for the cherubim he placed near the Ark, in the Holy of Holies of the Temple at Jerusalem (1 Kings, Chap. VI, verses 23-30). Those who relate the story of Saint Francis of Assisi, attribute this same form to the Angel who came to imprint on him the stigmata of the Passion.

Angelic apparitions did not, however, always take place in the same manner. It is said of the Angel who kept the gate of the earthly Paradise, after the expulsion of Adam and Eve, that he held in his hand a flaming sword, which turned every way, that is to say, according to the most probable interpretation, a peculiar kind of weapon, resembling a wheel with spokes of fire.

Moses again tells us that the cherubim in the Tabernacle, « stretched forth their wings on high, and covered over the Mercy Seat with them, with their faces one to another toward the Mercy Seat. »

View of Nazareth.

In the writings of Saint Paul, Saint Denis and other Fathers of the Church, the idea of angels is further worked out, and they are divided into various ranks, subordinate to each other, such as: hierarchies, orders, choirs; according to the degree of their glory, or the work appointed them to do.

In the sketch of Nazareth given here, the little town is seen from the escarpment overlooking it on the west, from which the Jews wished to throw Jesus down at the beginning of His Ministry. On the right can be seen the Sanctuary of the « Grotto of the Annunciation » and the « Casa Nova » of the Franciscans of the Holy Land.

In the centre rises the Mahommedan Mosque with its dome and minarets, occupying the site of the Synagogue where Jesus so often preached and performed so many of His miracles.

In the distance, towards the east, can be seen the summit of Mount Tabor, the scene of the Transfiguration, whilst, opposite to the spectator, rise the hills which surround the town, and which Jesus must often have crossed on His way to Cana lying beyond them, or to the shores of the Sea of Tiberias, which is in the same direction, near to which so great a part of His public life was passed.

The Vision of Saint Joseph

Saint Joseph seeks a lodging at Bethlehem
Saint Luke — Chap. 2.

ibant omnes, ut profiterentur singuli in suam civitatem.

4. Ascendit autem et Joseph a Galilæa de civitate Nazareth, in Judæam, in civitatem David, quæ vocatur Bethlehem, eo quod esset de domo et familia David;

5. Ut profiteretur cum Maria desponsata sibi uxore prægnante.

ND all went to be taxed, every one into his own city.

4. And Joseph also went up from Galilee, out of the city of Nazareth, into Judæa, unto the city of David, which is called Bethlehem (because he was of the house and lineage of David);

5. To be taxed with Mary his espoused wife, being great with child.

SAINT JOSEPH SEEKS A LODGING AT BETHLEHEM

THE NATIVITY OF OUR LORD AND SAVIOUR JESUS CHRIST

It is three days' walk, by the direct road from Nazareth to Bethlehem; and if you go by way of Jerusalem, four days are required.
    The travellers summoned to be taxed by the decree of Cæsar Augustus, when Cyrenius was Governor of Syria, must have been very numerous, and the one caravansary the town could boast, must have been quite insufficient to accommodate them all. As a matter of fact we must understand by the « diversorium » used in the Vulgate, a simple caravansary and not a regular hostelry properly so called, such as is implied in most French translations of the Gospels. The sort of establishment to which we apply the term of hostelry, or inn, would have been altogether foreign to the Oriental usages of the time under notice and this is still very much the case.

The Nativity of Our Lord and Saviour Jesus Christ
Saint Luke — Chap. 2

ACTUM est autem, quum essent ibi, impleti sunt dies ut pareret,

7. Et peperit filium suum primogenitum.

ND so it was, that while they were there, the days were accomplished that she should be delivered,

7. And she brought forth her firstborn son.

It will be well to say a few words about this town of Bethlehem where the first years of Our Saviour's childhood were passed.
    Bethleem or Bethlehem is also known by the Hebrew name of Ephrata. These words mean the « House of Bread » and « the land or country ».
    The Arabs give it another name resembling the first: for they call it Bait-Lahem, or the « House of Meat ».
    The origin of this town dates from the most remote antiquity. Moses speaks of it in the 35th chapter of Genesis in connection with the birth of Benjamin, which took place, he tells us, when his parents had but a little way to come to Ephrath (which is the same as Bethlehem), Rachel dying immediately afterwards.

The Nativity of Our Lord and Saviour Jesus Christ.

At the time of the Conquest of Palestine by Joshua, Bethlehem was, like Jerusalem, inhabited by the idolatrous Canaanites, and in the division of the conquered districts, it fell to the lot of the tribe of Judah.

The situation of Bethlehem, moreover, is most beautiful. Built on the crest of the mountains of Judæa, about two leagues to the south of Jerusalem, its form is that of a crescent, one end of which is marked by the Wells of David, the other by the Grottoes of the Nativity. Between the two horns of the crescent stretches a fertile valley, the Wady-el-Karoubeh. The descent of this valley is very steep, and resembles a circus, with low, parallel walls, which keep the earth from sliding down, representing the tiers of seats. This valley presents a most charming appearance, clothed, as it is, with an abundant vegetation, in which vines, fig, olive and almond trees abound.

The view from the top of the plateau is bounded on the north by the Hill of Mar-Elias, and on the west by the Mountains of the Desert where St. John dwelt. On the east, Beit-Saour rises from the little hill where Ruth gleaned the ears of corn in the field of Boaz, whilst beyond can be seen the sterile stony hills, called the Wilderness. Yet further to the east the rocks of Mount Moab stretch along like a wall, the base of which is bathed by the waters of the Dead Sea. On the south, Mount Herodion forms a regular cone, on the summit of which a few ruins indicate the site of the castle of Herod. It was here that the tetrarch was interred, and later, the Crusaders raised defensive works, hence its more modern appellation of the Hill of the Franks.

The Grottoes of the Nativity are a series of natural caves, extending for a considerable distance in the mountains, forming chambers connected with each other. As a matter of fact, shepherds, watching their flocks on the hills, availed themselves of these shelters in cold or bad weather, and it was in them that Mary and Joseph, finding no place in the caravansary, decided to take refuge.

The particular spot indicated by tradition is situated in the lower part of one of these caves, reached by two slopes, now converted into flights of stone steps.

Between the two sets of steps is a slight depression which tradition indicates as the spot to which Mary retired for the actual birth of the divine Child.

It was only after the birth that she carried Him a few paces further to a more commodious place, more sheltered from the cold, where it was possible to give the cave something of the semblance of a room.

There, says the legend, were some animals: an ox and an ass, but, however that may be, Mary found something there to serve the purpose of a crib, in which to lay her new-born child; this crib, or manger as it is generally called, is now preserved in the Church of Santa-Maria-Maggiore at Rome, where it is visited and venerated by numerous pilgrims.

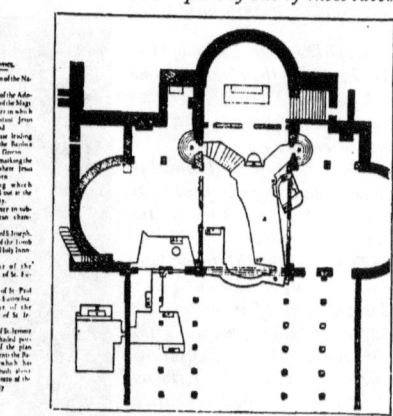

The Grotto of the Nativity at Bethlehem.   J.-J. T.

The place rendered sacred by the birth of the Saviour naturally became a goal of pilgrimage. The early Christians flocked to it in crowds. After the revolt of the Jews, under Barcocheba, the Emperor Hadrian had a temple to Jupiter erected on the Mount of Olives, on the very scene of the Ascension; a temple to Venus, on Golgotha; and one to Adonis, above the Grottoes of Bethlehem. These three temples remained standing for one hundred and eighty years, thus providentially attesting the sites of these venerated sanctuaries, until the time when Saint Helena, mother of the Emperor Constantine, replaced them with basilicas, in honour of Jesus Christ.

The Basilica of Bethlehem is still standing, and with the exception of the façade, which is hidden by massive buildings, is almost intact.

The interior consists of five naves, divided by rows of columns with Corinthian capitals, which were probably taken from the ruins of the Temple of Jerusalem, which was doubtless the source of much of the material used in the basilicas of St. Helena, erected in an extremely short space of time.

A Typical Jewish Armenian.

Gloria in Excelsis Deo
Saint Luke — Chap. 2

T pastores erant in regione eadem vigilantes, et custodientes vigilias noctis super gregem suum.

9. Et ecce angelus Domini stetit juxta illos, et claritas Dei circumfulsit illos, et timuerunt timore magno.

10. Et dixit illis angelus : Nolite timere ; ecce enim evangelizo vobis gaudium magnum, quod erit omni populo :

11. Quia natus est vobis hodie Salvator, qui est Christus Dominus, in civitate David.

ND there were in the same country shepherds abiding in the field, keeping watch over their flock by night.

9. And, lo, the angel of the Lord came upon them, and the glory of the Lord shone round about them : and they were sore afraid.

10. And the angel said unto them, Fear not : for, behold, I bring you good tidings of great joy, which shall be to all people.

11. For unto you is born this day in the city of David a Saviour, which is Christ the Lord.

12. Et hoc vobis signum : Invenietis infantem pannis involutum, et positum in præsepio.

13. Et subito facta est cum angelo multitudo militiæ cœlestis, laudantium Deum, et dicentium:

14. Gloria in altissimis Deo, et in terra pax hominibus bonæ voluntatis.

Gloria in Excelsis Deo.

12. And this shall be a sign unto you : Ye shall find the babe wrapped in swaddling clothes, lying in a manger.

13. And suddenly there was with the angel a multitude of the heavenly host praising God, and saying:

14. Glory to God in the highest and on earth peace, good will toward men.

The place where the shepherds were when the Angels appeared to them is supposed to have been what is now called Beit-Saour, a word signifying « the house of the Shepherds ».

This village is probably the ancient Chimham, alluded to by the Prophet Jeremiah (Chap. XLI, verse 17), where the people halted on their flight into Egypt, after the treacherous murder of Gedaliah by Ishmael, the son of Nathaniah.

It is surprising, at first sight, that shepherds should have been watching their flocks in the open air, at the time of year when Christ was born, for the cold must have been intense. It was, no doubt, to the end of December that the account in Holy Writ refers; but the pastures were not vast grazing grounds where the sheep were gathered together in thousands, from every direction, but mere local fields, where each shepherd tended his own little group of animals. And there is nothing in this to surprise any one familiar with the customs of the East. After the December rains are over, the grass begins to grow again, and the flowers reappear. Moreover, the severity of the winters varies very much, and some especially fine days occur, even in the very heart of the cold season, when the shepherds of Bethlehem would go down into the plain with their flocks, as the Arabs do in good seasons.

In England and Denmark, sheep are allowed to feed out of doors nearly all the winter, and Cicero tells us that the shepherds of Cicilia and Phrygia treated their flocks in a similar manner. In Mesopotamia, according to Genesis (Chap. XXXI, verse 40), the same custom prevailed, for Jacob said : « In the day the drought consumed me, and in the night the frost.»

Why should not the same custom have prevailed in Palestine, at the time of the birth of Christ? The Holy Land is not far from the countries we have just mentioned; the climate is certainly warmer than that of Europe, and even if we never see the same thing now, is not that readily explained by the changes that have taken place in the climate there, as elsewhere, a fact to which we shall have occasion to refer later.

The Adoration of the Shepherds

The Adoration of the Shepherds
Saint Luke — Chap. 2

T factum est, ut discesserunt ab eis angeli in cœlum, pastores loquebantur ad invicem: Transeamus usque Bethlehem, et videamus hoc verbum quod factum est, quod Dominus ostendit nobis.

16. Et venerunt festinantes, et invenerunt Mariam, et Joseph et infantem potitum in præsepio.

17. Videntes autem cognoverunt de

ND it came to pass, as the angels were gone away from them into heaven, the shepherds said one to another: Let us now go even unto Bethlehem, and see this thing which is come to pass, which the Lord hath made known unto us.

16. And they came with haste, and found Mary, and Joseph, and the babe lying in a manger.

17. And when they had seen it, they

verbo, quod dictum erat illis de puero hoc.

18. Et omnes qui audierunt, mirati sunt et de his quæ dicta erant a pastoribus ad ipsos.

19. Maria autem conservabat omnia verba hæc, conferens in corde suo.

made known abroad the saying which was told them concerning this child.

18. And all they that heard it wondered at those things which were told them by the shepherds.

19. But Mary kept all these things, and pondered them in her heart.

The Old Testament (Micah, Chap. IV, verse 8) refers to a « Tower of the flock, the stronghold of the daughter of Sion », which served as a refuge to the shepherds and their charges, in cases of nocturnal surprise. The Targum calls it the Tower of Eder, and prophesies that it will be on it that the Messiah will appear on the last day. We are, I think, justified in supposing it to have been the scene of the apparition of the angels, though there is no positive evidence on the point. Similar towers were to be seen in more than one place on hills in country districts. Even at the present day, the Arabs have recourse to such towers to protect them from the attacks of the Bedouins, but there was one special peculiarity of the shelters between Bethlehem and the Holy City, and that was, the rearing in them of the ewes, rams and young bulls, destined for the daily sacrifices of the Temple.

The Gospels tell us, that when the shepherds were surprised by the angels, they were « abiding in the fields, keeping watch over their flock by night ». The night was always divided into three so-called watches, the shepherds changing guard every three hours during the short night of the summer, and every four hours during the longer night of the winter. In the latter case, the first watch ended at ten, and the second at two, whilst the third lasted till daybreak. The shepherds on guard gathered round a camp fire, whilst waiting their turn to rest, and it must have been to those thus waiting that the angels appeared. They would, of course, wake their comrades, to tell them the wonderful news, after which they all went to Bethlehem, where they found and worshipped the Holy Child.

Presentation of Jesus in the Temple
Saint Luke — Chap. 2

T postquam impleti sunt dies purgationis ejus secundum legem Moysi, tulerunt illum in Jerusalem, ut sisterent eum Domino,

23. Sicut scriptum est in lege Domini :

ND when the days of her purification according to the law of Moses were accomplished, they brought him to Jerusalem, to present him to the Lord,

23. As it is written in the law of the

PRESENTATION OF JESUS IN THE TEMPLE

Quia omne masculinum adaperiens vulvam, sanctum Domino vocabitur;

24. Et ut darent hostiam secundum quod dictum est in lege Domini, par turturum, aut duos pullos columbarum.

25. Et ecce homo erat in Jerusalem, cui nomen Simeon, et homo iste justus et timoratus, exspectans consolationem Israel, et Spiritus sanctus erat in eo.

26. Et responsum acceperat a Spiritu sancto, non visurum se mortem, nisi prius videret Christum Domini.

27. Et venit in Spiritu in templum. Et quum inducerent puerum Jesum parentes ejus, ut facerent secundum consuetudinem legis pro eo,

28. Et ipse accepit eum in ulnas suas, et benedixit Deum, et dixit :

29. Nunc dimittis servum tuum, Domine, secundum verbum tuum in pace ;

30. Quia viderunt oculi mei salutare tuum,

31. Quod parasti ante faciem omnium populorum;

32. Lumen ad revelationem gentium, et gloriam plebis tuæ Israel.

33. Et erat pater ejus et mater mirantes super his, quæ dicebantur de illo.

34. Et benedixit illis Simeon, et dixit ad Mariam, matrem ejus: Ecce positus est hic in ruinam, et in resur-

Lord, Every male that openeth the womb shall be called holy to the Lord;

24. And to offer a sacrifice according to that which is said in the law of the Lord, a pair of turtledoves, or two young pigeons.

25. And, behold, there was a man in Jerusalem, whose name was Simeon ; and the same man was just and devout, waiting for the consolation of Israel : and the Holy Ghost was upon him.

26. And it was revealed unto him by the Holy Ghost, that he should not see death, before he had seen the Lord's Christ.

27. And he came by the Spirit unto the temple : and when the parents brought in the child Jesus, to do for him after the custom of the law,

28. Then took he him up in his arms, and blessed God, and said,

29. Lord, now lettest thou thy servant depart in peace, according to thy word :

30. For mine eyes have seen thy salvation,

31. Which thou hast prepared before the face of all people :

32. A light to lighten the Gentiles, and the glory of thy people Israel.

33. And Joseph and his mother marvelled at those things which were spoken of him.

34. And Simeon blessed them, and said unto Mary his mother, Behold, this child is set for the fall and

The Aged Simeon.

rectionem multorum in Israel, et in signum cui contradicetur;

35. Et tuam ipsius animam pertransibit gladius, ut revelentur ex multis cordibus cogitationes.

36. Eterat Anna prophetissa, filia Phanuel de tribu Aser : hæc processerat in diebus multis, et vixerat cum viro suo annis septem a virginitate sua.

37. Et hæc vidua usque ad annos octoginta quatuor; quæ non discedebat de templo, jejuniis et obsecrationibus serviens nocte ac die.

38. Et hæc, ipsa hora superveniens, confitebatur Domino, et loquebatur de illo omnibus qui exspectabant redemptionem Israel.

rising again of many in Israel, and for a sign which shall be spoken against;

35. Yea, a sword shall pierce through thy own soul also, that the thoughts of many hearts may be revealed.

36. And there was one Anna, a prophetess, the daughter of Phanuel, of the tribe of Aser : she was of a great age, and had lived with an husband seven years from her virginity;

37. And she was a widow of about fourscore and four years, which departed not from the temple, but served God with fastings and prayers night and day.

38. And she coming in that instant gave thanks likewise unto the Lord, and spake of him to all them that looked for redemption in Jerusalem.

The Presentation of Jesus in the Temple.

5

The Presentation of Our Saviour Jesus Christ in the Temple must have taken place at the top of the steps which led up from the Court of the Women (Azarath naschim) to the Court of the Men and to that of the Priests, where was the Altar of Burnt Sacrifice.

In the Court of the Women were five receptacles for offerings, which fact led to this court being called in the Gospels the « gazophylacium ». At certain hours services with singing and processions were performed in it. The Prophetess Anna who served God with fastings and

PRESENTATION OF JESUS IN THE TEMPLE

prayers night and day in the Temple evidently witnessed the *Presentation of Jesus*, which must have taken place in the morning according to the rules of the Temple.

In the background of my picture on p. 24 can be seen a terrace overlooking the court above the three entrance gateways, from which the women looked on at important ceremonies. On these occasions this terrace was supplemented by a kind of trellis-work balcony, which to some extent concealed from those outside what was going on. From this point of view the Altar of Burnt Offerings, the ceremonies of sacrifice, with other details of the services, could be seen between the intervening columns.

This arrangement left the Court of the Women vacant for the crowds of men who failed to find room in their own court, which as a matter of fact was not large enough to hold more than two thousand.

Below the terrace at the four corners of the Court of the Women were four chambers left open to the sky. In that on the south-west were kept the stores of oil and wine used in the Temple services; it was called the « Oil-Chamber». That on the south-east was reserved to the Nazarites or abstainers, where they had the pulse boiled which they had brought with them to offer in sacrifice. The Nazarites had to shave their heads and burn the hair thus cut off in the fire under the sacrifice on the Altar.

In the chamber at the northern corner of the Court of the Women the wood used in the sacrifices on the Altar of Burnt Offerings was sorted. Those Priests whose physical infirmities unfitted them for the service of the Altar were employed to inspect this wood and lay aside any of it which was worm-eaten. The fourth chamber, at the north-east corner, was reserved to Lepers.

The Court of the Women was entered on the east of the Temple by the Beautiful or Corinthian Gate; crossing this Court, which was about sixty-five and a half yards long, the worshipper found himself opposite the doorway, where, as we have already stated, the presentations took place. It was reached by a semi-circular staircase of fifteen steps, corresponding with the fifteen Psalms called the «Degrees» chanted one on each step during the libations.

These steps were very low; three taken together only gave a height of half a cubit, so that the whole fifteen steps represented but two and a half cubits, which gives a total height of about four and a half feet. It is Josephus who gives us these details, and they help us to understand the legend, telling how Mary when presented in the Temple at the age of three years, cleared all the steps at one bound. This, which would have been impossible with an ordinary staircase, would thus really have been a very simple matter.

This fact quite escaped the painters who have followed the legend in their treatment of the subject of the Presentation of the Virgin, as Tintoretto did in his picture in the Venetian Academy.

The greater number of those who have endeavoured to restore the plan of the Temple of Herod place the Nicanor Gate between the Court of the Women and that of the Men, at the head of the semi-circular staircase of the fifteen steps or of the Psalms, of which we have just spoken. They indicate on the east, as the Entrance to the Court of the Women, the Beautiful or Corinthian Gate, spoken of in the Acts of the Apostles in the account of the healing of the lame man by Saint Peter and Saint John.

On this last point they are right; but they ignore what is nevertheless certain, that the three names: Beautiful, Corinthian and Nicanor all denote one and the same entrance. The Talmud, in fact, in the Midoth Treatise, places the Nicanor Gate exactly on the site of the Beautiful or Corinthian Gate, and it agrees on this point with Josephus. This remark seems to us to throw a new light on the commentary on the passage in the Acts of the Apostles which we have just quoted.

The actual gates of the Gateway in question were of Corinthian brass, hence the name of Corinthian Gate. They were brought from Alexandria by a certain Nicanor and it is said miraculously saved from shipwreck. This was the only Gateway not overlaid with plaques of gold, because, as the Talmud tells us, the brass of which it was made itself gleamed as brightly as gold; hence the name of Beautiful. The gates, it adds, were so heavy that it took eighteen Levites to close them. We must make allowance here of course for the exaggeration so habitual in the Talmuds.

Lastly, on the rampart enclosing the sacred enceinte of the Temple there were pillars of marble, on which were inscriptions threatening with death any heathen who should dare to pass the limits prescribed by them. One of these pillars, discovered by M. Clermont-Ganneau in a house in Jerusalem, is actually now in the Constantinople Museum, and the Hebrew Museum of the Louvre in Paris has a cast of it.

The Magi on their Journey
Saint Matthew — Chap. 2

Cuum ergo natus esset Jesus in Bethlehem Juda in diebus Herodis regis, ecce Magi ab Oriente venerunt Jerosolymam,

2. Dicentes : Ubi est qui natus est rex Judæorum ? vidimus enim stellam ejus in Oriente, et venimus adorare eum.

Now when Jesus was born in Bethlehem of Judæa in the days of Herod the king, behold, there came wise men from the east to Jerusalem,

2. Saying, Where is he that is born King of the Jews? for we have seen his star in the east, and are come to worship him.

The Book of Daniel speaks of Magi or soothsayers who were in the service of King Nebuchadnezzar, who studied astronomy and interpreted dreams. Those referred to in the Gospels seem to have been not only wise men, but Kings or Sheiks of Chaldea and its neighbourhood. They too were addicted to the study of the heavenly bodies and perhaps also worshipped them, which explains the immediate attention they accorded to a sign appearing in the heavens at

the moment of the birth of the Messiah. The colour of their undergarments, which was yellow, indicated their profession.
What was the star referred to in the sacred record? There is absolutely no positive evidence on this point. Some think it was a comet or some other similar body. Others are of opinion that it was a meteor resembling more or less a shooting star, which trailed slowly along at a little distance from the ground, so as actually to guide the steps of the Magi. The Gospel seems to sanction the latter interpretation when it says : the star « came and stood over where the young child was », a star properly so called would not have indicated the spot with such precision. However that may be, it is clear that the significance of the sign was revealed in some way to the Magi. The prophecy of Balaam to which reference is generally made does not appear sufficiently precise. Balaam merely said: « There shall come a star out of Jacob» and, judging from the context, the word star is evidently used in a figurative sense, so that it could only give a very vague indication, quite insufficient to explain the determination of the Magi.
Had the travellers exchanged ideas previous to their arrival? It is very probable that they had. No doubt their caravans, though they started from different points, met beyond the Jordan, on the side of the Mountains of Moab, whence they entered the Promised Land, still preceded by the star. This is the moment represented in my picture. The district they are crossing is near the Holy City; it shews the volcanic hills on the shores of the Dead Sea, between Jericho, the Kedron valley and Jerusalem.

The Wise Men and Herod

Saint Matthew — Chap. 2

AUDIENS autem Herodes rex, turbatus est, et omnis Jerosolyma cum illo.

4. Et congregans omnes principes sacerdotum et scribas populi, sciscitabatur ab eis ubi Christus nasceretur.

5. At illi dixerunt ei : in Bethlehem Judæ; sic enim scriptum est per prophetam :

6. Et tu Bethlehem, terra Juda, nequaquam minima es in principibus Juda ; ex te enim exiet dux, qui regat populum meum Israel.

WHEN Herod the king had heard these things, he was troubled, and all Jerusalem with him.

4. And when he had gathered all the chief priests and scribes of the people together, he demanded of them where Christ should be born.

5. And they said unto him, In Bethlehem of Judæa : for thus it is written by the prophet,

6. And thou Bethlehem, in the land of Juda, art not the least among the princes of Juda : for out of thee shall come a Governor, that shall rule my people Israel.

The Magi on their way to Bethlehem.

Interview of the Magi with Herod.

7. Tunc Herodes, clam vocatis Magis, diligenter didicit ab eis tempus stellæ quæ apparuit eis.

8. Et mittens illos in Bethlehem, dixit : Ite et interrogate diligenter de puero ; et quum inveneritis, renuntiate

7. Then Herod, when he had privily called the wise men, enquired of them diligently what time the star appeared.

8. And he sent them to Bethlehem, and said, Go and search diligently for the young child; and when ye have found

| mihi, ut et ego veniens adorem eum. | him, bring me word again, that I may come and worship him also. |
| 9. Qui quum audissent regem, abierunt. | 9. When they had heard the king, they departed. |

The advisers consulted by Herod belonged to the Sanhedrim, the supreme national tribunal of the Jewish people. This Sanhedrim consisted of seventy-one members divided into three classes, or, as we should say now, chambers. The first chamber consisted of the Chief-Priests, also called Princes, who either were or had been in office, and the heads of the twenty-four sacerdotal families; the second included the scribes and doctors of the law, and the third the elders or notable men of the Jewish nation.

The Adoration of the Magi
Saint Matthew — Chap. 2

T ecce stella quam viderant in Oriente, antecedebat eos, usque dum veniens staret supra, ubi erat puer.

10. Videntes autem stellam, gavisi sunt gaudio magno valde.

11. Et intrantes domum, invenerunt puerum cum Maria, matre ejus, et procidentes adoraverunt eum; et apertis thesauris suis, obtulerunt ei munera, aurum, thus et myrrham.

ND, lo, the star, which they saw in the east, went before them, till it came and stood over where the young child was.

10. When they saw the star, they rejoiced with exceeding great joy.

11. And when they were come into the house, they saw the young child with Mary his mother, and fell down, and worshipped him: and when they had opened their treasures, they presented unto him gifts; gold, and frankincense, and myrrh.

The word « house » used by the Evangelist to indicate the place where the Magi found the Messiah seems to point to the conclusion that, during the journey of their visitors from the east, Joseph and Mary had left the Cave of the Nativity for a more comfortable dwelling. Tradition is, however, rather against this idea; but it must be remembered that with regard to this event in the life of Jesus traditional accounts vary very greatly. The Gospel narrative has become the nucleus of a mass of legends in which popular imagination has revelled. Nothing is certain either as to the number or names of the Magi. According to Saint Leo and Saint Gregory of Arles they were three in number, thus symbolizing the three persons of the Trinity and the three sons of Noah. The three gifts offered naturally led to this belief. Other less numerous accounts, however, increase sometimes even to twelve the number of the worshippers of the Infant Jesus. A legend of the Eastern Church relates that they were accompanied by a suite of a thousand attendants and that they had left beyond the Euphrates an army of seven thousand combatants (Saint James of Edessa). Their names are very variously given. Some call them : Bithisarea, Melchior and Gathaspar; others : Magalath, Panganath, and Saracen, yet others : Appellius, Amerius and Damascus; but the names almost unanimously adopted by Oriental tradition are those we meet with in the well-known verse of ancient liturgy :

Gaspar fert myrrham, thus Melchior, Balthasar aurum.

Peter of Natalibus makes the three Magi twenty, forty and sixty years old respectively, and the Venerable Bede goes so far as to describe them, quoting from a tradition of his day, telling us that Melchior, old and pale, with long white hair and beard, offered gold to the Saviour as King; whilst Gaspar, the second wise man, a beardless youth with a rosy complexion, offered incense as a gift worthy of God, and the third, Balthasar by name, shadowed forth by the gift of myrrh the fact that the Son of Man was to suffer death. These types have been generally adopted by the artists of Western Europe.

The monk Cyril and John of Phocas say that two miles from Bethlehem there was a cave where the Magi rested after the adoration of the Holy Child and where they were warned of God in a dream not to return to Herod.

The Massacre of the Innocents
Saint Matthew — Chap. 2

Tunc Herodes, videns quoniam illusus esset a Magis, iratus est valde. Et mittens occidit omnes pueros, qui erant in Bethlehem, et in omnibus finibus ejus, a bimatu et infra, secundum tempus quod exquisierat a Magis.

17. Tunc adimpletum est quod dictum est per Jeremiam prophetam, dicentem :
18. Vox in Rama audita est, ploratus, et ululatus multus : Rachel plorans filios suos, et noluit consolari, quia non sunt.

Then Herod, when he saw that he was mocked of the wise men, was exceeding wroth, and sent forth, and slew all the children that were in Bethlehem, and in all the coasts thereof, from two years old and under, according to the time which he had diligently enquired of the wise men.

17. Then was fulfilled that which was spoken by Jeremy the prophet, saying,
18. In Rama was there a voice heard, lamentation, and weeping, and great mourning, Rachel weeping for her children, and would not be comforted, because they are not.

THE MASSACRE OF THE INNOCENTS

The account of this horrible massacre astonishes many readers of the Gospel narrative and they exclaim that it is improbable. It must, however, be remarked that the number of children under two years old in Bethlehem and its neighbourhood is not likely to have exceeded sixty. What were a hundred murdered children to Herod? There were nothing but butcheries throughout his reign, and even his own family was not safe from his fury. According to the Emperor Augustus: it was better to be Herod's pig than his son; and Voltaire says that Nero was gentle compared to this tyrant. Of the six children born to him he killed four. After the siege of Jerusalem the members of the Sanhedrim were all massacred. Antigonus conquered; he was killed; Aristobulus, Herod's brother-in-law, was drowned in his bath; the venerable Hyrcanus, the last of the Asmonæans or Maccabees, was murdered; Herod's wife Mariamne was assassinated, his last two sons, her children, were strangled; the two leaders of revolts, Judas and Matthias, were burnt alive, with many others of less note. When he felt his own death approaching, Herod ordered the massacre of thirty thousand Jews in the circus of Jericho in honour of his funeral.

According to tradition, the Massacre of the Innocents took place in the following manner: all the mothers who had children under two years of age were gathered together, under the pretext of a fête to be held in honour of the birth of one of Herod's own sons. Not a mother would have liked to miss it, and all the poor women came, bringing their little ones decked out in their best. To avoid a tumult when the broken-hearted mothers gave vent to their shrieks of despair on discovering the cruel deception, the women were made to enter one by one a porch opening into a court. There the child was torn from the mother's arms and flung into the gloomy court, whilst she was driven out at the other end of the porch or gallery, so that the group of waiting mothers, still in happy ignorance and eager for their own turn to come, had no suspicion of what awaited them.

The Childhood of John the Baptist
Saint Luke — Chap. 1

PUER autem crescebat, et confortabatur spiritu; et erat in desertis usque in diem ostensionis suæ ad Israel.

AND the child grew, and waxed strong in spirit, and was in the deserts till the day of his shewing unto Israel.

Tradition indicates as the desert in which the child who was to be called the «Prophet of the Highest» spent his early years, that on the west of Aïn-Karim, amongst the rugged rocks skirting the Terebinth valley. It was from the bed of the torrent which flows through this valley that David took the stones for the sling with which he went forth to meet and slay Goliath. There grew the so-called locust-tree or Saint John's bread-tree with various shrubs and roots, and there, too, were plenty of the locusts and wild honey which we are told formed the food of the Prophet. The Rabbi Hanina B. R. Abahon mentions eight hundred varieties of «locusts» which are good to eat.

About the middle of this desert a cave is still shewn as that occupied by the Prophet, near a spring called Ain-Habise. In the fifteenth century the hills of this desert were still, as in the days of David and of the Prophet John, covered with dense woods, but now they are bare and, except in the rainy season, the streams which flowed through the numerous ravines are dried up.

John the Baptist paid his first visit to the Desert and spent some time in it with his mother Elizabeth after the Massacre of the Innocents. Later, probably after the death of his parents, he returned to it to prepare for his mission.

The Flight into Egypt
Saint Matthew — Chap. 2

UI quum recessissent, ecce angelus Domini apparuit in somnis Joseph, dicens: Surge, et accipe puerum et matrem ejus, et fuge in Ægyptum, et esto ibi usque dum dicam tibi. Futurum est enim ut Herodes quærat puerum ad perdendum eum.

ND when they were departed, behold, the angel of the Lord appeareth to Joseph in a dream, saying: Arise, and take the young child and his mother, and flee into Egypt, and be thou there until I bring thee word; For Herod will seek the young child to destroy him.

14. Qui consurgens, accepit puerum et matrem ejus nocte, et secessit in Ægyptum.

14. When he arose, he took the young child and his mother by night, and departed into Egypt.

The Flight into Egypt.   J. J. T.

To get to Egypt the Holy Family, after leaving Bethlehem, must have gone by way of Hebron or Bersabea where there remains to this day a little mosque dedicated by the Mussulmans to «Saint Joseph the carpenter» in memory of the passage of the Holy Family. From it

a distant view can be obtained of the mountain slopes, and of the Mediterranean Sea near Gaza. It was in this direction that the fugitives bent their steps. They must have entered Egypt by way of Pelusium and have reached Heliopolis and then the Egyptian Babylon, where old

THE CHILDHOOD OF SAINT JOHN THE BAPTIST

Digitized by Google

Cairo now stands. We will indicate further on the route taken by the Holy Family on their way back from Egypt.

The Sojourn in Egypt

The Sojourn in Egypt.   J.-J. T.

T erat ibi usque ad obitum Herodis, ut adimpleretur quod dictum est a Domino per prophetam dicentem : Ey Ægypto vocavi filium meum.   s. matth. — cap. 2.

ND was there until the death of Herod: that it might be fulfilled which was spoken of the Lord by the prophet, saying, Out of Egypt have I called my son. s. matthew — ch. 2.

The Church of the Copts in Old Cairo (the ancient Egyptian Babylon) is one of the very oldest Christian churches of Egypt. It dates from the sixth century, and was built above a cave or kind of natural crypt, which is reached at the present day by a few steps, and in which, according to tradition, the Holy Family took shelter during their exile.

The little Babylonian colony was a very busy one at the time of which we are writing, and there must have been many dahabeahs laden with corn and other produce on the banks of the Nile, with crowds of fellahs occupied about them.

The water of the Nile, though rather muddy, was good, and was used for drinking and other domestic purposes by the inhabitants. At certain hours of the day the women went in long files to draw water at a very convenient part of the port, and the very spot is still shewn where the Virgin often came, carrying the Infant Jesus in her arms. Indeed, it seems likely that Mary would be very unwilling, especially in a foreign land, to leave her divine son alone; moreover Joseph, occupied as he was with his trade of a carpenter, would probably be frequently absent. It will be remembered that he was employed, at least so tradition says, in making the woodwork used in Egyptian houses, especially the wainscotting so much in vogue in Egypt.

Beyond the spot just mentioned, and in the background of my picture, can be seen the island of Rhodes, sacred to the memory of Moses, for it is said that it was on it that he was found amongst the flags by the daughter of Pharaoh.

Another goal of pilgrimage, and one of the most venerated of all the spots connected with the sojourn in Egypt, is near the town of Heliopolis. This is the so-called sanctuary of Matareeh, where, according to tradition, the Virgin, weary with her long journey, rested beneath the shade of a sycamore tree. The tree itself is no longer there, but a shoot from it, dating from about the fifteenth century, still marks the spot. Here, says the legend, the heat being great, the Virgin was thirsty, and a spring gushed forth for her refreshment; hence the name of Matareeh, which signifies clear water, given to the venerated site.

At Heliopolis, if yet another tradition is to be believed, the idols in a temple suddenly fell down when the Holy Family passed.

The Return from Egypt
Saint Matthew — Chap. 2

EFUNCTO autem Herode, ecce angelus Domini apparuit in somnis Joseph in Ægypto,

20. Dicens : Surge, et accipe puerum et matrem ejus, et vade in terram Israel ; defuncti sunt enim qui quærebant animam pueri.

21. Qui consurgens, accepit puerum et matrem ejus, et venit in terram Israel.

UT when Herod was dead, behold, an angel of the Lord appeareth in a dream to Joseph in Egypt,

20. Saying, Arise, and take the young child and his mother, and go into the land of Israel : for they are dead which sought the young child's life.

21. And he arose, and took the young child and his mother, and came into the land of Israel.

THE RETURN FROM EGYPT

The journey into Egypt, with the rest of the events of the childhood of Jesus, has given rise to a multitude of more or less curious legends. In this case, as in every other, the Oriental imagination has proved itself fertile in inventions, some of them charming, others grotesque, and the Apocryphal Gospels are simply full of them.

According to some of these stories the souls of the Holy Innocents appeared in the air in bodily form on the departure of the Infant Saviour for His exile and accompanied Him throughout the journey. When He was hungry, the trees, it is said, bent down of themselves to offer Him their fruit; springs of water gushed out at His feet to quench His thirst, and Angels appeared to Him, as young children, to amuse Him with their dancing and singing. On the way back it was the birds who fêted His passage, accompanying Him and flying round His head. Even the robbers were converted from their evil ways, or at all events, did Him homage, and amongst them, it is said, was the thief who was later to be crucified with the Lord and forgiven by Him.

All these legendary tales are of course but of little importance; what concerns us more is to ascertain, if possible, what was the age of Jesus on His return from Egypt. Scholars are not at all agreed on this point. Some say He was three, others five, others again seven and yet others nine years old. As for us, we are free to confess that in following the last quoted, we have chosen, not so much the opinion which seemed in itself the most probable, but the one which pleased us best. The question at issue is, as will readily be understood, not exactly of vital importance from our particular point of view; and, by choosing to consider that the Holy Child was nine years old, we have gained an element of interest and variety which we should have been very sorry to lose.

We know for a fact that the Infant Jesus was one year old when He started for Egypt. Now, according to the historian Josephus, Herod died a few days after the murder of Antipater, and therefore not long after the Massacre of the Holy Innocents, as Macrobius has pointed out. It follows therefore that Jesus was not more than two years in Egypt; for

The Citadel of Cairo. View taken from Mount Mokatam.

we know that He was taken there one year before the death of Herod, and, according to the Gospel account, returned very soon after that event, when Archelaus was reigning in Judæa.

The return of the Holy Family was doubtless far less fatiguing than the journey to Egypt. In the first place the Holy Child was older and the road was now a little better. On leaving

The Return from Egypt.   J.-J. T

or OldCairo to go towards Pelusium, the travellers first traversed sandy districts, passing salt marshes, and then followed the coast by way of Gaza and Jaffa, till they entered Samaria. There they left the open country, and made their way through the numerous valleys beyond it and came to Jenin, whence they entered and crossed the Plain of Esdraelon. Nazareth, for which they were bound, was then quite near, beyond a few mountain spurs. The journey probably occupied about seven days.

Jesus and His Mother at the Fountain
Saint Luke – Chap. 2

T ut perfecerunt omnia secundum legem Domini, reversi sunt in Galilæam, in civitatem suam Nazareth.

40. Puer autem crescebat, et confortabatur, plenus sapientia, et gratia Dei erat in illo.

ND when they had performed all things according to the law of the Lord, they returned into Galilee, to their own city Nazareth.

40. And the child grew, and waxed strong in spirit, filled with wisdom : and the grace of God was upon him.

In the Holy Land there are a certain number of wells, called Wells of the Virgin Mary

(Aïn-sitti Mariam). The most celebrated is that of Siloam, situated on the south-east of the Temple, in the Valley of Jehoshaphat. This was the well which partly supplied with water the Pool of Siloam, to which Jesus Christ sent the man who had been born blind to purify himself after He had given him sight by anointing his eyes with clay made by mixing earth with His own spittle.

Another of these wells is that of Aïn-Karim. It is situated near what is known as the Desert of John the Baptist. According to tradition, the Virgin Mary went to this well during her visit to Elizabeth whose house was near it. Yet another is shewn at Nazareth, which is evidently the one to which the Holy Virgin went most frequently, and according to a Greek legend, it was there that the Angel Gabriel first appeared to her who was to be the Mother of the Redeemer, to prepare her to receive him on his later mission, when he was to give her his more definite and, so to speak, official message.

In our picture, the Holy Child wears the garment without seam, made of a kind of woven linen of a purplish brown colour. The legend about this garment is well known. It tells how Mary wove it herself for her son, and that it grew with His growth, so that it lasted Him until the time of His passion and death. Over the seamless garment Jesus wears what was called a « gibbeh », a loose robe open at the neck, kept in place by a sash which He wore as a Jew of pure descent, for it was part of the Rabbinical law that the upper or nobler part of the human body should be thus separated from the lower.

Jesus and His Mother at the Fountain. J.-J.T

Jesus lost
Saint Luke — Chap. 2

T quum factus esset annorum duodecim, ascendentibus illis Jerosolymam secundum consuetudinem diei festi.

ND when he was twelve years old, they went up to Jerusalem after the custom of the feast.

43. Consummatisque diebus, quum redirent, remansit puer Jesus in Jerusalem, et non cognoverunt parentes ejus.	43. And when they had fulfilled the days, as they returned, the child Jesus tarried behind in Jerusalem; and Joseph and his mother knew not of it.
44. Existimantes autem illum esse in comitatu, venerunt iter diei, et requirebant eum inter cognatos et notos.	44. But they, supposing him to have been in the company, went a day's journey; and they sought him among their kinsfolk and acquaintance.
45. Et non invenientes, regressi sunt in Jerusalem, requirentes eum.	45. And when they found him not, they turned back again to Jerusalem, seeking him.

Was this the first time Jesus had been with His parents to the Feast of Pentecost? The Gospel does not say that it was, and the probability is that it was not. Every Jew was commanded (see Exodus XXIII, verse 14, and Deuteronomy XVI, verse 16) to go up three times a year to the Tabernacle and later to the Temple, and above all « to keep the feast of unleavened bread ». Fear of Archelaus alone would have kept the Holy Family back, and it is not likely that that prevented them for any length of time from fulfilling a precept of the law, the keeping of which they had so much at heart.

The Gospel tells us that the parents of Jesus waited till they had « fulfilled the days » to return to Nazareth. This they were not compelled to do by Jewish law, which could not have required so long a sojourn at Jerusalem. The Feast of Pentecost, in fact, lasted seven whole days, and on this occasion they must have remained for the whole of it, before starting for home.

Mount Mokatam. View taken from the Citadel of Cairo.

According to one tradition, it was at Beeroth, the modern El Bireh, an hour and a half's march from Jerusalem, that the Holy Virgin and Saint Joseph noticed that Jesus was no longer with them. Great crowds of Galileans must have been returning from Jerusalem, one *huge caravan succeeding another, each made up of natives from one part of the country. At the first issue from the Holy City, the various parties would, of course, get mixed together, but they divided into groups, growing ever smaller and smaller as the people branched off at the various cross roads. No doubt Joseph and Mary thought Jesus had stayed behind with friends in the rear of their own caravan. Full of anxiety Mary and Joseph went a little further, probably to Jifnah, the first halting-place, and there waited, but the Child did not appear. Then they turned back to Jerusalem seeking Him. A few years ago a tree was still shewn at Jifnah which, according to a tradition of the country, marked the spot where Mary halted twice : once going to, and once returning from, Jerusalem.*

Jesus amidst the Doctors
Saint Luke — Chap. 2

T factum est, post triduum invenerunt illum in templo, sedentem in medio doctorum, audientem illos et interrogantem eos.

47. Stupebant autem omnes qui eum audiebant super prudentia et responsis ejus.

ND it came to pass, that after three days they found him in the temple, sitting in the midst of the doctors, both hearing them, and asking them questions.

47. And all that heard him were astonished at his understanding and answers.

Saint Luke tells us that Jesus was found in the Temple after three days. We must not, however, conclude that He had remained there for three whole days. This mode of expression, which is several times used in the Gospels, simply means that He was found on the third day, counting as the first day of His absence that on which the first stage of the journey was performed after leaving Jerusalem, before He was missed and on the evening of which His parents sought Him « amongst their kinsfolk and acquaintance and found Him not » ; the second day was that needed for the return to Jerusalem, whilst the third was doubtless that on the morning of which they found Him in the Temple, sitting in the midst of the doctors. This calculation resembles that by means of which the passage in the same Gospel is explained referring to the body of Jesus having remained in the sepulchre three days, which cannot possibly mean three times twenty-four hours, as is clearly proved by other passages of the sacred text.

The time passed by Jesus in the Temple is not likely to have been all spent in talking with the doctors; a considerable portion of it would doubtless have been passed in prayer, and the Priests are certain to have supplied Him with food, so that He was not obliged to ask for it as a charity.

It is not known with any certainty in what part of the Temple the interview with the doctors took place. On the left of the Court of the Men and on the south of the Temple, was a spacious chamber assigned to purposes of teaching, but, as it was reached by way of the Court of the Men, women could not enter it. They could only take part in ceremonies, etc., from a distance, by climbing into the walled-in balcony to which we referred above, and which was over the cloisters surrounding the Women's Court. If, therefore, Jesus was found with the doctors in this chamber, it is possible that Mary and Joseph first saw Him through the railings, but they could not have spoken to Him then in the manner they did. It is therefore more likely that it was in the Cloisters of the Court, near the entrance, that the groups of doctors with Jesus were found by His parents, the Holy Child sitting in their midst « both hearing them and asking them questions », so that « all they that heard Him were astonished at His understanding and answers ».

What was the subject of this discussion? It is impossible to say with any certainty. According to the fancy of certain sainted personages it was about medicine, the healing properties of plants,

Jesus lost.

and the structure of the human frame. According to others it was astronomy, the system to which our earth belongs, etc. All this is of course mere guess work, but after all very possible. The doctors of the Temple occupied themselves with all manner of questions, for it must be remembered that amongst the Jews all knowledge was looked upon as sacred, and the Priests were the only learned men and teachers. There were, therefore, amongst them doctors of medicine, astronomers, specialists in every branch of science, each one famed for his skill in one or another branch of knowledge. There would then have been nothing surprising in the fact that face to face with this remarkable Child, Whose answers astonished all who heard them, each specialist should have amused himself by putting to Him enquiries about the subjects he had himself mastered. From this would result a vast number of questions, lengthening out the time occupied in the interview.

Cloisters of the Mehemet Ali Mosque.

If there be one absolutely legitimate conjecture on the subject, it is surely that expressed by many great doctors of the Church, to the effect that the question of the expected Messiah is not likely to have been passed over in silence. In fact, it is very evident that Jesus did not go to the Temple to talk with the learned men of Israel for mere pleasure, or for the sake of shewing off His own supernatural knowledge. His only aim must have been to prepare them more or less directly for His future mission. Now it appears to have been necessary for the end in view, to enlighten their minds as to what the true nature of the Messiah was and the time when He should manifest Himself. The prophecies concerning Him would therefore have to be recalled and explained by the Saviour, even as He explained them later, on the way to Emmaus, for the instruction of His disciples. He probably called their attention to the fulfilment of the seventy weeks of the prophet Daniel (Dan. IX, verse 24) and reminded them of the passing of the kingdom of Israel into the hands of a foreigner, which was to be a sure sign of the imminent advent of the Messiah. By this means our Lord's future teaching, confirmed by His miracles, would be better understood and be more likely to be accepted.

It is not, however, necessary to suppose that the meeting of doctors referred to in the Gospel was specially convened by Jesus on His arrival at the Temple. Such meetings often took place, especially at the great Feasts, for instance, at that of Pentecost, or on the Day of Atonement. The Bible was then read aloud and, no doubt, commented upon. The Talmud gives us the curious detail that, if the High Priest should fall asleep during the reading, he was to be woke up, not by calling him by name, or by touching him on the shoulder, but by snapping the thumb and the middle finger close to his ears.

Jesus sitting in the midst of the Doctors.

Jesus Found
Saint Luke — Chap. 2

T videntes admirati sunt. Et dixit mater ejus ad illum : Fili, quid fecisti nobis sic ? Ecce pater tuus et ego dolentes quærebamus te.

ND when they saw him, they were amazed; and his mother said unto him, Son, why hast thou thus dealt with us ? behold, thy father and I have sought thee sorrowing.

THE HOLY CHILDHOOD

49. Et ait ad illos : Quid est quod me quærebatis? nesciebatis quia in his quæ Patris mei sunt, oportet me esse ?
50. Et ipsi non intellexerunt verbum quod locutus est ad eos.

49. And he said unto them, How is it that ye sought me? wist ye not that I must be about my Father's business?
50. And they understood not the saying which he spake unto them.

The Women's Court, where, as already stated, the meeting between Jesus and His parents probably took place, was of considerable size and adjoined that of the men. It was reached, as we said above, by a semi-circular staircase on which the Levites, bearing harps, dulcimers, cymbals and other instruments of music, chanted the fifteen Psalms called the Songs of the Degrees. During the offering of sacrifices they chanted near the Altar.

In the background of the picture through the door can be seen the Altar of Burnt Offerings; a red band was painted all round it to indicate where the sprinklings with blood were to cease. These sprinklings, which took place constantly, both within and without the veil upon the Mercy seat and before it, were performed with three fingers, much in the same way as a blow with a rod is given, the blood had to be sprinkled from right to left. The blood was received in a basin of gold with a handle, and the bottom of this basin was round, so that there should be no temptation to the Priest to rest it on the ground, for the blood had to be constantly kept moving, lest it should congeal and thus become unfit for the purpose for which it was required. These perpetual sprinklings so stained the veil of the Sanctuary that when Titus took it to Rome it was completely encrusted with dry blood.

In the Priests' Court, which was on the north of the Altar of Sacrifice, there was often such a quantity of blood that something like stepping stones were provided to save the inmates from having to wade knee deep in it.

Of course when the Temple was built, provision was made for the draining away of all this blood. It escaped through a groove or channel surrounding the Altar, and on the eastern side were two openings called the « nozzles » which, the Talmud tells us, led to the very depths. No

Haram: Mosque of Es-Sakhra, called the Mosque of Omar, Jerusalem.   J.-J. T.

doubt the blood was finally lost in the numerous subterranean passages opening into the vast quarries which, on the side of the Gate of Damascus, extended beneath the whole of the Temple site. It was to these subterranean passages that eighty thousand young men of the tribe

JESUS FOUND

of Levi fled when Jerusalem was taken by Nebuchadnezzar. They were all burnt and their remains buried beneath the ruins of the Temple.

We may conveniently give here a few more curious details, culled from the Talmudic writings, of the way in which the sacrifices in the Temple were offered. The crowds of assistants were divided into various groups, the foremost of which entered the Men's Court. The gates were then closed and the officiating Priests sounded the trumpets, first blowing a short sharp note, then a prolonged and, so to speak, rounded one, and then yet another short one. These Priests were divided into two distinct rows, those in the first being provided with silver basins, whilst those in the second had golden ones. The two sets of Priests always kept separate, never mixing with each other.

Typical Jews.

The lay Israelite was allowed to slaughter his lamb, but this was the only part of the ceremony in which any but a Priest could take an actual share. The lamb slain, the Priest received the blood in the vessel he held, passed it to his neighbour in the same row, and it was handed along thus, till it came back in a similar manner empty. The Priest nearest the Altar, having received the basin full of blood, poured it out in the stream on the north-west side, taking care not to touch the Altar itself and not to spill a single drop. When the first row of Priests had completed their sacrifice, the second row took their places, and so on.

The Altar of Burnt Offerings was wiped every Friday with a linen cloth and white-washed once a year. The number of victims immolated was enormous; about three hundred thousand lambs alone being offered up every year. The Jews were accustomed to these hecatombs. The Talmud tells us that in the time of the Kings, so many wild asses were killed to feed the lions kept in the Royal menageries that the blood flowed in streams through the streets, so that the Israelites who came up to Jerusalem for the great feasts waded in it ankle deep.

The Youth of Jesus

Saint Luke — Chap. 2

T descendit cum eis, et venit Nazareth; et erat subditus illis. Et mater ejus conservabat omnia verba hæc in corde suo.

52. Et Jesus proficiebat sapientia et ætate et gratia apud Deum et homines.

ND he went down with them, and came to Nazareth and was subject unto them: but his mother kept all these sayings in her heart.

52. And Jesus increased in wisdom and stature, and in favour with God and man.

THE HOLY CHILDHOOD

The Gospels tell us nothing of the occupations of Jesus as a young man. Tradition relates and it appears truly, that He followed the profession of Saint Joseph. Some say that He spent the whole thirty years before He began His ministry in retirement, leading a kind of monastic life devoted entirely to prayer; but nothing could be less probable. Later, the Gospels relate that the people of Nazareth, who must have known Him well, seeing that He had passed His life amongst them, asked « Is not this the carpenter's son? » It would indeed have been very extraordinary and altogether out of keeping with the spirit of the rest of His life if Jesus had not helped Saint Joseph with his work, contributing to the support of His family, whose circumstances were humble, and setting the example of a useful life to those whom He was later to teach. Saint Paul, even when he became a preacher, continued to practise the craft of a tent-maker, so as not to be a charge to the faithful, and it seems only natural that Christ Himself should have done no less than His Apostles, for, to quote His own words, « The Son of Man came not to be ministered unto but to minister. »

As for all the charming anecdotes accumulated in the Apocryphal Gospels, such as the pretended miracles of Jesus in His childhood, birds restored to life, stones endued with animation, pieces of wood lengthened to save Saint Joseph trouble, and so on, they are, one and all, altogether unworthy of the slightest credit. The Gospels assert positively that the first miracle performed by Jesus was that at the marriage feast at Cana of Galilee, and, had the Apocryphal accounts been true, it would be impossible to understand how the Son of God could have lived in the quiet way that He did before His public ministry; whilst the incredulity of His own cousins, who had been witnesses of how He spent the first thirty years of His life, would be equally incomprehensible. There can be no doubt that all these early miracles, had they taken place, would have drawn public attention upon Him and rendered impossible the plan of His Heavenly Father, Who willed that His Son should remain unknown amongst men until the hour predetermined by Him.

Equally erroneous are the assertions of others as to the studies of Jesus, the pretended journeys with a view to becoming initiated in the wisdom of the Egyptians and of the people of India. Jesus had no master; there was no one who could teach Him anything, and His fellow countrymen may well have been astonished at the divine wisdom He displayed when they exclaimed : « How knoweth this man letters, having never learned ? » (St. John, VII, verse 15.)

The special idea of the picture called « The Youth of Jesus » is the following : As already stated, Jesus practised the trade of a carpenter, or some other similar to it, and in the course of His daily work He must sometimes have performed actions foreshadowing certain details of the tragic and bloody drama which was to terminate His earthly career. It is improbable, especially after the prophecy of the aged Simeon, that Joseph and Mary had no inkling of what the future of their Child was to be. With some such inkling in their minds the smallest detail, a mere nothing, would be enough to arouse their anxiety and sadden them. We have imagined some such incident : Jesus is carrying a piece of wood on His shoulder ; whilst Mary and Joseph watch Him thoughtfully with some vague presentiment of the future Cross.

Bas-relief from the El-Aksa Mosque.

EXPLANATORY NOTES

(1) Page 8 : « The Holy Ghost shall come upon thee and the power of the Highest shall overshadow thee. »

That is to say, that Jesus, the true Son of God, and God Himself, was to become incarnate in the womb of Mary by means of a pure miracle of the almighty power of God, without the intervention of man, and therefore without violation of the virginity of His mother. (Cornel. a Lap., Menochius, and all Catholic commentators.)

(2) Page 17 : « Mary brought forth her firstborn Son. »

According to the general acceptation in the Bible, the word firstborn *simply signifies here that Mary had had no other son before the birth of Jesus, but it does not at all imply that she had no other sons later. (Cornel. a Lap., Menochius, etc.)*

(3) Page 24 : « That the thoughts of many hearts may be revealed. »

That is to say, that the evil disposition of the enemies of Jesus shall then be made manifest. (Menochius, etc.)

(4) Page 43 : « Jesus grew and waxed strong in spirit, filled with wisdom, and the grace of God was upon Him. »

As He grew in age He gradually gave proof of the infinite treasures of wisdom and of grace which were in Him from the beginning. (Cornel. a Lap., Menochius, etc.)

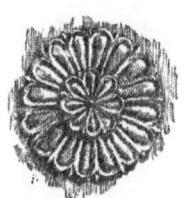

THE MINISTRY

Jewish Ornament.

INTRODUCTION

HAT portion of the life of Jesus during which He taught the people was not in itself the most important, but from the point of view of the painter who wishes to portray Him under many different aspects it is the richest in varied and characteristic episodes. The baptism, the temptation, the calling of the Apostles, the teaching in the Synagogue, the journeys to and fro, rich in miracles and sublime incidents, the actual preaching, interspersed with so many striking parables, and supplemented by the gestures and movements of the crowds to whom those parables were told, all these things combine to call up a series of vivid pictures, every page of the Gospels, even when merely read, filling the mind with emotion and enthusiasm. Such was the subject I had now to render, and I must say a few words to explain how I understood it.

As I have already explained in my Introduction to these volumes as a whole, my one aim is to interpret Jesus. Now Jesus is a very complex individuality, for He is both God and man, and even if treated as man only He has many aspects, for He is alike the type of humanity as a whole and of the Jewish race in particular. He is the hero of one century and at the same time the master spirit of all ages. I had to give a rendering of Him in each and all of these manifold aspects, and I had but one medium with which to perform my task : that of my art. For, truth to tell, I am not a literary man, I am a painter. Instead of a consecutive discourse, in which the truth is gradually unfolded, I have at my disposal but a series of successive pictures, each illustrating some one aspect of our Lord's career. It is not for me to say whether this be an advantage or a disadvantage, all that is certain is that the pictorial mode of expression, the only one at my command, imposed on me one rigorous condition : that of having to make my own choice of subjects.

I have, then, chosen from amongst the scenes of the public life of Jesus, those which best illustrate not only what He is, but what He was, and what He ought to be to us; especially those which, being more suggestive than others, are a better starting-point for the imagination in its efforts to rise to the comprehension of that incomprehensible ideal which is the Christ. The episodes and parables of the Gospels, in which the heart of the Master was laid bare, and in which His thoughts, His designs, His temporary and eternal relations with Humanity were revealed; such were the subjects which first claimed my attention. Then, anxious to make Jesus known as a typical member of a peculiar race at a special epoch of its history, I set myself to seek scenes in which full justice could be done to historical truth and local colouring. From this quest resulted certain compositions of which at first sight the *raison d'être* is not perhaps apparent. They are intended to put the spectator in touch with contemporary Jewish civilisation at the time of the Roman domination; to bring vividly before him the people and their institutions, the country and its customs, in the midst of which the life of Christ was passed, so that, without too great a strain on his imagination, he may be able to form a just idea of what that life as a whole really was instead of adopting some one or another of the modern travesties of it evolved by the caprice of this or that critic.

It will now be understood why my pictures illustrative of the Parables are interspersed amongst my scenes from the actual life of Jesus, instead of being grouped separately. Had I followed the latter plan, not only would a certain heaviness and monotony have been the result, but I should also have misled the public as to my intentions, for it would have seemed as if I wished to give a series of illustrations of the *teaching* of Jesus, which is not the case. I only wished to recall that teaching in those instances in which it reflected the personality of the Master, or the social environment in which He lived. For instance, I have represented the *Sower*, the *Good Samaritan*, the *Good Shepherd*, the *Vine* and the *Fig-tree*, because beneath all these figures Jesus Christ revealed Himself. Other parables, such as that of the *Blind leading the Blind when both shall fall into the ditch*, the two *Women grinding at the mill* and the *Son of the Lord of the Vineyard*, gave me an opportunity of painting on the spot some bit of natural scenery or some characteristic aspect of life in the East. If at the same time I saw a chance of embodying in any picture some great moral truth I was not slow to avail myself of it. As cases in point, I may mention the pictures of the *Man that layeth up treasure for himself*, the *Beggar Lazarus* and the *Pharisee and the Publican*.

Is it necessary for me to add that in all my compositions I have endeavoured, in addition to their historic and picturesque aspects, to render the philosophical side of the subject? For example, in the various synagogues I have painted, I have purposely accentuated the details of construction and ornamentation accumulated beyond measure by Jewish formalism; I have brought into relief the complex and complicated costumes of the rabbis, which are a reflection of the customs observed by them. In the midst of what I may call all this superannuated decorative lumber, the noble simplicity of the personality and doctrine of Christ stands out all the more vividly; we already foresee that He is come « not to destroy but to fulfil the law »; that He will sweep away all these mouldy accumulations of centuries; and we can understand the better the bitter hatred which the Divine reformer will arouse against Him on every side.

I will not, however, pursue this analysis too far; that would be to depart from my true rôle, and would really be a sign of weakness; for a work of art should need no commentary : every intelligent and attentive spectator ought to be able to grasp its meaning at once. My only wish in all I have just said is to arouse attention.

It may be asked why I have given separate portraits of Jesus, the Apostles and the other chief persons mentioned in the Gospels. Some will perhaps remark that it would have been enough to introduce them in the various scenes represented, and that as the portraits must of necessity be mere arbitrary representations, to give them by themselves was perfectly useless. I have not felt myself in the least bound to respect this objection. It was my earnest endeavour to obtain a distinct idea of every personality with whom I came in contact by the way; and I wanted to embody that idea. Penetrated by what the Gospels tell us of the lives, the moral temperaments, the acts of our Lord and His followers, I endeavoured to embody each personality in what I may call a synthetic portrait, in which the type alone was arbitrary, not either the character or the expression. Have I succeeded? I dare not venture to say; the enterprise was, it will be admitted, difficult enough, especially with regard to the divine figure which should dominate every other, that of Our Lord and Saviour Jesus Christ. In His case I had to give myself up to protracted meditation and prayer, and to appeal to every source of emotion at my disposal; yet after all the result seems to me to be but feeble.

Lastly, I have supplemented the principal compositions with a few sketches and studies taken on the spot, which I think introduce an element of agreeable variety in the work as a whole, and complete the story told by the paintings.

May I now in a few words answer certain criticisms which have been pronounced upon me? I set aside, of course, those which merely dwell upon the amount of talent shewn by my work; these, by the way, are rare, for the public and my brother artists have been very generous in their treatment of me. There are, however, certain remarks of another character which touch me far more nearly, and which I feel it my duty to reply to with a few observations.

It has been said : the work is not summary enough ; there are too many details, too many pictures; it would have been better to condense the whole into a few profound pages. I beg leave to differ from this opinion. As to profundity; well, I have sought it to the best of my ability; perhaps without attaining it; but it was my firm determination to be diffusive. And what proves to me that I was in the right is the difficulty that certain persons have from the first had in looking at things from the point of view I wished them to take. It is not easy to represent at the present day the environment in which Jesus lived; many things in attempted restorations of extinct civilisations astonish and even repel us. This being so, was it not of vital importance for me to take complete possession of the imagination of the spectator, to isolate him entirely from his preconceived ideas and to lead him slowly, yet without fatigue, along the paths where he will meet the true Christ? To have acted differently, under pretence of avoiding repetition, would, I think, have been to diminish my chances of success and to have exposed myself to being only half understood.

It has also been said, and this has wounded me alike as a believing Christian and as an artist with convictions of my own : what was the good of painting Christ like that? The only Christ there is any sense in painting now-a-days is the Christ crowned with thorns; that is to say a conventional Christ, such as the devout are used to; Christ as you conceive Him to have been is no longer a subject for the painter, for nobody believes in Him now.

To this I reply, to begin with : that, as for me, I believe in Him firmly, and that, consequently, I have every right to express my own conviction in my own way. I then answer that it is not true that nobody believes in Christ at the present day; what is more near the truth is, that He is ignored and forgotten, which is precisely what gives me confidence in the opportuneness of my work. I wished to say to this positive century, whether it is presumption on my part I know not, this it appears to me is what once happened in the history of humanity. This is what I have read; what you too can read for yourselves in history, not in a history concocted after consulting some system, but in true history, sincere history, disinterested and courageous history. Now, what took place then is worth thinking about! The whole of human life depends on it; in it we can find what we all so earnestly seek in this century, what has been sought in all past centuries : help, comfort, light, ideality, hope of eternal happiness. Once more, was it for me to speak of these things? I do not know, but it does seem to me that it is permitted to every one to interest himself in his fellow men, to endeavour loyally and simply with the help of the resources at his command, to lead them back to what he thinks is the truth, when he sees them disregarding or forgetting, yet still needing it.

Such was my thought: it seems to me good. The sincere public shall be the judge of the result.

Ossuary. J.-J. T.

THE MINISTRY

Union in Prayer
Saint Matthew — Chap. 18

MEN dico vobis quæcumque alligaveritis super terram, erunt ligata et in cœlo, et quæcumque solveritis super terram, erunt soluta et in cœlo.

19. Iterum dico vobis, quia si duo ex vobis consenserint super terram, de omni re, quamcumque petierint, fiet illis a Patre meo, qui in cœlis est.

20. Ubi enim sunt duo vel tres congregati in nomine meo, ibi sum in medio eorum.

Union in Prayer.   J.-J. T.

ERILY I say unto you, Whatsoever ye shall bind on earth shall be bound in heaven : and whatsoever ye shall loose on earth shall be loosed in heaven.

19. Again I say unto you, That if two of you shall agree on earth as touching any thing that they shall ask, it shall be done for them of my Father which is in heaven.

20. For where two or three are gathered together in my name, there am I in the midst of them.

As a frontispiece to our book we have a representation of « Jesus shewing Himself through the lattice », a subject which seemed to us to symbolize in a striking manner the manifestation of Jesus Christ to the souls of men in the Gospels. Here, following the Gospel record itself, we give a rendering of a thought which serves as a complement to the first; that is to say, we shew the gathering together of several souls and their union with each other and the Lord through the reading in common of the Holy Scriptures.

The Voice in the Desert
Saint John — Chap. 1

IXERUNT ergo ei : Quis es, ut responsum demus his qui miserunt nos ? Quid dicis de te ipso ?

23. Ait : Ego vox clamantis in deserto : Dirigite viam Domini, sicut dixit Isaias propheta.

S. MATTH. — CAP. 3

3. Hic est enim qui dictus est per Isaiam prophetam dicentem : Vox clamantis in deserto : Parate viam Domini, rectas facite semitas ejus.

HEN said they unto him, Who art thou? that we may give an answer to them that sent us. What sayest thou of thyself?

23. He said, I am the voice of one crying in the wilderness, Make straight the way of the Lord, as said the prophet Esaias.

ST. MATTHEW—CH. 3

3. For this is he that was spoken of by the prophet Esaias saying, The voice of one crying in the wilderness, Prepare ye the way of the Lord, make his paths straight.

The Voice in the Desert.

The Desert in which dwelt John the Baptist was three hours' march from Jerusalem, the Terebinth valley shutting in and isolating it. Opposite to it on the west, when the back was turned on Aïn-Karim where Elizabeth dwelt, could be seen on the lofty mountains the villages and towns of Kastoul, perched on a hilltop; Kalounieh, further away in the valley on the right; Soba, scarcely visible in the distance and looking like an eagle's nest, with Shathaf, and other hamlets upon the slopes. It was in the wider portion of this valley that so many struggles took place between the Israelites and Philistines, and it was there that Goliath was killed, smitten in the forehead by the stone from the sling of David.

In these rocky valleys the voice resounds in an extraordinary manner, and even now the traveller is struck with the way in which the long drawn-out melancholy cries of the shepherds ring out in the silent solitudes. The voice echoes back from side to side to a very great distance. Now it so happened that in the fifteenth year of the reign of Tiberius Cæsar an unusual and exciting incident occurred again and again at the close of the day, for a voice, a strange appealing voice, resounded through the silence and the gathering shades of night : « Prepare ye the way of the Lord, make His paths straight », « the Saviour, the Messiah is near », « repent ye, for the kingdom of Heaven is at hand ». This mysterious chanting probably went on till the night was well advanced. It was known that a human being lived alone in the desert, a prophet, no doubt, and the voice having now been heard for some time, people in Jerusalem and the villages round about became curious as to what it might mean, so that groups began to collect and to venture to approach the place from which it came. These groups presently found themselves face to face with a remarkable being, leading a most mysterious life and apparently altogether possessed with the thought of some great approaching event. John the Baptist then began to preach in the wilderness; the crowd ever increasing, when he drew the people after him till he came to the banks of the Jordan, where he baptized many. If we want to get a true idea of the extent of John the Baptist's influence we have only to read what he said to the leaders of the people : the Pharisees and Sadducees. He treated them with an independence and addressed them in terms of a character so strong and searching, that they would never have been tolerated in the mouth of an ordinary man.

The Ax laid unto the root of the Tree
Saint Matthew — Chap. 3

Facite ergo fructum dignum pœnitentiæ.

9. Et ne velitis dicere intra vos : Patrem habemus Abraham; dico enim vobis quoniam potens est Deus de lapidibus istis suscitare filios Abrahæ.

10. Jam enim securis ad radicem arborum posita est. Omnis ergo arbor quæ non facit fructum bonum, excidetur et in ignem mittetur.

Bring forth therefore fruits meet for repentance :

9. And think not to say within yourselves, We have Abraham to our father : for I say unto you, that God is able of these stones to raise up children unto Abraham.

10. And now also the ax is laid unto the root of the trees: therefore every tree which bringeth not forth good fruit is hewn down, and cast into the fire.

The Ax laid unto the root of the Tree.

11. Ego quidem baptizo vos in aqua in pœnitentiam; qui autem post me venturus est, fortior me est, cujus non sum dignus calceamenta portare. Ipse vos baptizabit in Spiritu sancto et igne.

11. I indeed baptize you with water unto repentance : but he that cometh after me is mightier than I, whose shoes I am not worthy to bear; he shall baptize you with the Holy Ghost, and with fire.

A useless tree or one which is ornamental only is a rare thing in the East. The fields of the owners of the soil are not bordered with plantations of trees as with us, and every tree which bears no fruit is soon cut down to be used for one or another purpose : for building, in carpentry, for making tools or for fuel, whilst the copses beyond the cultivated districts and the clumps of trees by the wayside, have all their special meaning. The olive and fig-trees, which are the species of most frequent occurrence, are not preserved for the sake of their fruit alone, for their foliage affords a grateful shade and a valuable protection from the heat of the sun. In the solitudes where the flocks are taken to graze, the isolated trees are a shelter alike during the hot hours of the day and in storms. The chief isolated trees in the Holy Land are the so-called Saint John's bread-tree, the sycomore and the mulberry. In the case of a tree growing near a well or some spot sacred to prayer, there would be a chance of its life being respected and spared, but unless some such evidently useful purpose served it as a safeguard, it was sure to perish. Every passer by would think he had a right to appropriate it to himself; each one would cut off and carry away a branch and it would not long continue to cumber the ground.

He who fans his wheat
Saint Matthew — Chap. 3

Cujus ventilabrum in manu sua; et permundabit aream suam; et congregabit triticum suum in horreum, paleas autem comburet igni inextinguibili.

Whose fan is in his hand, and he will thoroughly purge his floor, and gather his wheat into the garner; but he will burn up the chaff with unquenchable fire.

In the towns and villages of the East the fanning of the wheat alluded to in the Gospel narrative may still often be seen. In the evening when a breeze is beginning to blow and

THE WINNOWER

sometimes in the morning, when the weather is favourable, men with wooden shovels may be seen on the house tops «fanning» or winnowing their wheat. The wheat is tossed in the air in a large cloth, the wind carries away the husks and dust whilst the good grain remains to be heaped up on the roof.

It is in the evening, too, that the inhabitants of the towns and villages sit outside their doors in the narrow streets and chat together. Some of the women go down to the well in little groups, whilst others spread out on the roof to dry the bright, many-coloured garments and the carpets they have washed. The traveller passing through the streets at this time has often some difficulty in making his way, for he is jostled at every turn by some group of idlers taking the air.

Mountains near Jericho.

As it is now, so it has ever been in the East, so that at the time when John the Baptist was preaching the picture called up by him of the fanner of the wheat must have been perfectly familiar to the imagination of his hearers. Moreover, the comparison of the righteous and the wicked to good grain and chaff is of frequent occurrence in the Gospels; and it is indeed a forcible one when we remember the little store set on the husks flung carelessly in the air and dispersed by the wind, as contrasted with the very great value of the good grain.

Saint John the Baptist and the Pharisees
Saint Luke — Chap. 3

T interrogabant eum turbæ, dicentes : Quid ergo faciemus?

11. Respondens autem dicebat illis : Qui habet duas tunicas, det non habenti ; et qui habet escas, similiter faciat.

12. Venerunt autem et publicani ut baptizarentur, et dixerunt ad illum : Magister, quid faciemus?

ND the people asked him, saying, What shall we do then?

11. He answereth and saith unto them, He that hath two coats, let him impart to him that hath none ; and he that hath meat, let him do likewise.

12. Then came also publicans to be baptized, and said unto him, Master, what shall we do?

Saint John the Baptist and the Pharisees

13. At ille dixit ad eos : Nihil amplius quam quod constitutum est vobis faciatis.

14. Interrogabant autem eum et milites, dicentes : Quid faciemus et nos ? Et ait illis : Neminem concutiatis, neque calumniam faciatis, et contenti estote stipendiis vestris.

13. And he said unto them, Exact no more than that which is appointed you.

14. And the soldiers likewise demanded of him, saying, And what shall we do ? And he said unto them, Do violence to no man, neither accuse any falsely ; and be content with your wages.

We are able to form a very good idea of the noble way in which John the Baptist fulfilled his mission in the Desert. Every class of Jewish society flocked to consult him. As the man sent from God to preach penitence to the people, it was necessary for him to know what must be done to avert the calamities he prophesied. Each one who came to him wished to learn the secret of how to escape the judgment threatening his generation, and to each and all John had the right advice ready, the advice suited to the character and position of the enquirer.

It was natural that so energetic and important a preacher should attract the attention of the religious authorities; and therefore, probably at the initiative of the High Priest, Pharisees were sent from Jerusalem to enquire into his doctrine.

Saint John the Baptist sees Jesus from afar
Saint John — Chap. 1

T ego vidi; et testimonium perhibui quia hic est Filius Dei.

35. Altera die iterum stabat Joannes, et ex discipulis ejus duo.

36. Et respiciens Jesum ambulantem, dicit : Ecce agnus Dei.

ND I saw, and bare record that this is the Son of God.

35. Again the next day after John stood, and two of his disciples.

36. And looking upon Jesus as he walked, he saith, Behold the Lamb of God!

At Bethabara, the place where John the Baptist for the first time bore witness to Jesus, the Jordan is wider and not so deep as at its mouth, its waters divide there and it is more often fordable. It was here that the twelve stones were set up, marking the spot where the Children

of Israel crossed the Jordan, dryshod, to enter the Promised Land. There too David, fleeing from Absalom, passed over the river; whilst later it must have been here, or near here, that Elijah smote the waters with his mantle « so that they divided hither and thither », when « he and his companion went over on dry ground ».

· The Baptism of Jesus
Saint Matthew — Chap. 3

unc venit Jesus a Galilæa in Jordanem ad Joannem, ut baptizaretur ab eo.

14. Joannes autem prohibebat eum, dicens : Ego a te debeo baptizari, et tu venis ad me?

15. Respondens autem Jesus, dixit ei : Sine modo : sic enim decet nos implere omnem justitiam. Tunc dimisit eum.

16. Baptizatus autem Jesus, confestim ascendit de aqua, et ecce aperti sunt ei cœli, et vidit Spiritum Dei descendentem sicut columbam, et venientem super se.

17. Et ecce vox de cœlis dicens : Hic est Filius meus dilectus, in quo mihi complacui.

hen cometh Jesus from Galilee to Jordan unto John, to be baptized of him.

14. But John forbad him, saying, I have need to be baptized of thee, and comest thou to me?

15. And Jesus answering said unto him, Suffer it to be so now : for thus it becometh us to fulfil all righteousness. Then he suffered him.

16. And Jesus, when he was baptized, went up straightway out of the water : and, lo, the heavens were opened unto him, and he saw the Spirit of God descending like a dove, and lighting upon him :

17. And lo a voice from heaven, saying, This is my beloved Son, in whom I am well pleased.

The Divine Majesty of Jehovah was no longer made manifest in the second Temple; the stone which once upheld the Ark of the Covenant was vacant; the « urim » and the « thummim » had long been silent. But now once more the Divine Majesty reveals Himself and consecrates the Messiah on the banks of the Jordan. Twice more in the life of the Saviour will a similar manifestation take place; once on Mount Tabor at the Transfiguration and once in the Temple on the Wednesday of Passion week.

According to the early Gnostics it was at the moment of our Lord's baptism that the celestial Eon or first emanation from the Divinity which they call the Christ, descended upon Jesus and made Him divine. The Ebionites, in their turn, say that at the moment of the Lord's baptism a fire suddenly fell from Heaven and set fire to the waters of the Jordan.

THE BAPTISM OF JESUS

Jesus taken up into an high Mountain
Saint Luke — Chap. 4

ESUS autem plenus Spiritu sancto regressus est a Jordane, et agebatur a Spiritu in desertum...

5. Et duxit illum diabolus in montem excelsum...

ND Jesus being full of the Holy Ghost returned from Jordan, and was led by the Spirit into the wilderness...

5. And the devil, taking him up into an high mountain...

Tradition indicates Mount Nebo, one of the heights overlooking the mountains of Moab beyond the Dead Sea, as the high mountain to which Jesus was carried in the Temptation. It was to this same mountain that Moses had retired to die, and on it his body, which was never found, was miraculously buried.

Mount Nebo commands a very wide-stretching view and from it the tempter could easily have pointed out to our Lord the various directions of all those kingdoms which he offered to Him if He would fall down and worship him.

Truth to tell, the language employed in the Gospel narrative seems to imply something more than an ordinary view of an ordinary panorama. « He sheweth Him » it says « all the kingdoms of the world and the glory of them », but what this vision really was we do not know.

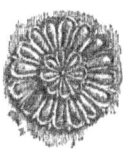

Jesus taken up into an high Mountain. L.-J. T.

Jesus tempted in the wilderness.

Jesus tempted in the Wilderness
Saint Luke — Chap. 4

ESUS autem plenus Spiritu sancto regressus est a Jordane, et agebatur a Spiritu in desertum
2. Diebus quadraginta; et tentabatur a diabolo. Et nihil manducavit in diebus illis, et consummatis illis, esuriit.
3. Dixit autem illi diabolus: Si Filius Dei es, dic lapidi huic ut panis fiat.
4. Et respondit ad illum Jesus:

ND Jesus being full of the Holy Ghost returned from Jordan, and was led by the Spirit into the wilderness,
2. Being forty days tempted of the devil. And in those days he did eat nothing : and when they were ended, he afterward hungered.
3. And the devil said unto him, If thou be the Son of God, command this stone that it be made bread.
4. And Jesus answered him, saying,

JESUS TEMPTED IN THE WILDERNESS

| Scriptum est : Quia non in solo pane vivit homo, sed in omni verbo Dei. | It is written, That man shall not live by bread alone, but by every word of God. |

    In many sanctuaries of the East, ostrich eggs are hung up. These eggs are often much ornamented and are supposed to be symbolic of certain Biblical allusions which they are intended to recall.

    The ostrich, it is said, broods over its eggs forty days, hence the idea of using it as a symbol of those events related in the Holy Scriptures, in which the number forty occurs. Now, such events are numerous. For instance, the Bible tells us that the flood was forty days and forty nights upon the earth; Joseph mourned forty days for his father in Egypt; Goliath defied the Jews for forty days before he was attacked and killed by David; and the Israelites were prepared for the entry into the Promised Land by forty years' wandering in the wilderness.

    In the life of Jesus the same number also occurs very frequently. Thus, He was presented in the Temple forty days after His birth; He was excommunicated from the Synagogue forty days before His Passion; He ascended to Heaven forty days after His death, and lastly, His Church has instituted a Lent of forty days in memory of His forty days' fast in the wilderness.

    The Gospel tells us in fact that, before beginning His public ministry, Jesus wished to prepare Himself

Jesus set upon a pinnacle of the Temple.

for it by forty days of fasting and prayer. Tradition fixes the scene of His retirement in a cave on a mountain which has received the name of Quarantania, round about which lie numerous stones, not unlike loaves of bread in shape, from which has arisen the idea accepted by many that it was such stones as these that the Devil referred to when he said « if Thou be the Son of God, command that these stones be made bread. »

    In the background of my picture, and on the other side of the Dead Sea, can be seen Mount Nebo, referred to in my last note, rising above the chain of heights known as the Mountains of

Moab. The rows of trees in the plain mark the course of the Jordan, and the town of Jericho, the ruins of which are so well known, was a little farther to the right.

It is remarkable with what devotion the early Christians observed the prolonged fast of their Divine Master. They made most earnest efforts to follow His example, and really sometimes succeeded in a wonderful way. Lucianus tells us that many of them went without a morsel of food for ten days at a time, and Saint Gregory Nazianzen asserts that the monks living in the solitudes of Pontus in Asia Minor, where he had a congregation under his care, prolonged this entire abstinence from food to the twentieth day. Saint Augustine (Epistle 86) speaks of having known Christians who fasted for more than a week at a time, and of having heard from credible witnesses of one person at least who succeeded in holding out to the fortieth day. According to the testimony of Theodoret, this was the case with Saint Simeon Stylites, who fasted for forty days every year.

Jesus set upon a pinnacle of the Temple

Saint Luke — Chap. 4

т duxit illum in Jerusalem, et statuit eum super pinnam templi, et dixit illi : Si Filius Dei es, mitte te hinc deorsum.

ND he brought him to Jerusalem, and set him on a pinnacle of the temple, and said unto him, If thou be the Son of God, cast thyself down from hence :

10. Scriptum est enim : Quod angelis suis mandavit de te, ut conservent te,

11. Et quia in manibus tollent te, ne forte offendas ad lapidem pedem tuum.

12. Et respondens Jesus ait illi : Dictum est : Non tentabis Dominum Deum tuum.

13. Et consummata omni tentatione diabolus recessit ab illo usque ad tempus.

10. For it is written, He shall give his angels charge over thee, to keep thee :

11. And in their hands they shall bear thee up, lest at any time thou dash thy foot against a stone.

12. And Jesus answering said unto him, It is said, Thou shalt not tempt the Lord thy God.

13. And when the devil had ended all the temptation, he departed from him for a season.

Our Saviour's body was carried in a passive condition by Satan above the Temple lit up by the rising sun. At His feet was the Court of the Women with its semi-circular staircase having on either side of the steps the entrances to the rooms where the musicians of the Temple kept their instruments. On that part of the building which dominated the Gate giving entrance to the Men's Court, above the flights of steps known as the Psalms or Songs for the reason already explained, Herod had a golden eagle placed as a compliment to the Imperial Government. This led to very serious troubles; some young men having had the hardihood to throw down in broad daylight what they looked upon as an idol. Farther away, the Antonia Tower or Citadel, occupied by a garrison of Roman soldiers, dominated the Temple. In the angle of the Court of the Women, shewn in my picture, can be seen one of the chambers open to the sky, already described as occupying the four corners. This is the Leper's Chamber, the other three, it will be remembered, were the Nazarite's Chamber, and the store rooms for the wine, oil and wood, used in the services of the Temple.

In our engraving, behind the figure of the Evil one, can be seen the Gateway of the Porch of the Temple. It was twenty cubits wide by forty high, and its lower half was hidden, as already described, by the Babylonian veil or curtain of four colours. The upper portion of the gateway, above this veil, was open to the air, so that the fumes of the incense burnt within the Holy Place escaped without difficulty.

This wide gateway was constructed in a very peculiar manner. It had no vault to complete and consolidate it, and its architect employed instead five beams of oak, separated from each other by rows of stones, each beam projecting on either side one cubit beyond that beneath it. To connect the façade with the wall of the Holy Place, great beams serving as stays were introduced inside the upper part of the Porch, and in the Porch itself hung chains of gold, with the aid of which novices, training for the priesthood, were able to swing themselves up and scale the wall, so as to reach the openings looking into the Holy Place. They could then see whether the crowns placed in rows to mask the windows were in good order and in their proper places.

Saint John.   J.-J. T.

In this same porch, before the golden gate of the Holy Place, which gate was a double door of somewhat complicated construction, there was a golden vine on which were suspended ornaments, such as olives and grapes, brought as votive offerings by those who wished to present gifts to the Temple. There were such quantities of these ornaments that, as we are told by Rabbi Eleazer, son of Rabbi Juda, three hundred novices were needed to carry away all the gifts and relieve the vine of the enormous weight of gold.

Jesus ministered to by Angels
Saint Matthew — Chap. 4

unc reliquit eum diabolus, et ecce angeli accesserunt et ministrabant ei.

hen the devil leaveth him, and, behold, angels came and ministered unto him.

Saint Mark — Chap. 1

13. Et erat in deserto quadraginta diebus et quadraginta noctibus, et tentabatur a Satana, eratque cum bestiis, et angeli ministrabant illi.

13. And he was there in the wilderness forty days, tempted of Satan; and was with the wild beasts; and the angels ministered unto him.

CALLING OF SAINT ANDREW AND SAINT JOHN

Angels came and ministered unto the Saviour and in some mysterious way renewed His powers. The strength given to Him did not result from the revival of bodily vigour through the natural means of partaking of food and drink; the help sent down from Heaven to fortify Him for the Mission He was about to undertake came from the same divine source as the manifestation which had taken place at His baptism. The forty days' retirement was thus inaugurated by one of the three manifestations from on high which proclaimed our Lord to be the Son of God and revealed His spiritual grandeur; and it closed with yet another heavenly manifestation, this time consecrating His body.

Such, at least, is our interpretation of the Gospel narrative. We do not pretend to force our point of view on others, the sacred text rather permits than enforces it, but we have preferred to consider the subject in its supernatural aspect rather than, as most painters have done, to make the Angels offer the Son of God a dish of dates, pomegranates, or figs. « Man doth not live by bread alone. »

Saint Peter and Saint Andrew.

The Calling of Saint Andrew and Saint John
Saint John — Chap. 1

LTERA die iterum stabat Joannes, et ex discipulis ejus duo.
36. Et respiciens Jesum

GAIN the next day after John stood, and two of his disciples;
36. And looking upon Jesus

ambulantem dixit: Ecce agnus Dei.

37. Et audierunt eum duo discipuli loquentem, et secuti sunt Jesum.

38. Conversus autem Jesus et videns eos sequentes se, dicit eis: Quid quæritis? Qui dixerunt ei: Rabbi (quod dicitur interpretatum Magister), ubi habitas?

39. Dicit eis: Venite et videte. Venerunt et viderunt ubi maneret, et apud eum manserunt die illo; hora autem erat quasi decima.

40. Erat autem Andreas frater Simonis Petri unus ex duobus, qui audierant a Joanne et secuti fuerant eum.

41. Invenit hic primum fratrem suum Simonem, et dicit ei: Invenimus Messiam (quod est interpretatum Christus).

as he walked, he saith, Behold the Lamb of God!

37. And the two disciples heard him speak, and they followed Jesus.

38. Then Jesus turned, and saw them following, and saith unto them, What seek ye? They said unto him, Rabbi, (which is to say, being interpreted, Master,) where dwellest thou?

39. He saith unto them, Come and see. They came and saw where he dwelt, and abode with him that day for it was about the tenth hour.

40. One of the two which heard John speak, and followed him, was Andrew, Simon Peter's brother.

41. He first findeth his own brother Simon, and saith unto him, We have found the Messias, which is, being interpreted, the Christ.

Saint Andrew.   J.-J. T.

Calling of Saint Peter and Saint Andrew
Saint Matthew — Chap. 4

MBULANS autem Jesus juxta mare Galilææ, vidit duos fratres, Simonem, qui vocatur Petrus, et Andream fratrem ejus, mittentes rete in mare (erant enim piscatores).

19. Et ait illis: Venite post me, et faciam vos fieri piscatores hominum.

20. At illi continuo relictis retibus secuti sunt eum.

ND Jesus, walking by the sea of Galilee, saw two brethren, Simon called Peter, and Andrew his brother, casting a net into the sea: for they were fishers.

19. And he saith unto them, Follow me, and I will make you fishers of men.

20. And they straightway left their nets, and followed him.

The Lake of Gennesaret near the site of Bethsaida.   J-J.T.

This time we are not told that Peter and Andrew were in their fishing boats, but that they were casting a net into the sea. This net was of the kind now called a sweep-net, and on the north of the Sea of Tiberias the shores are peculiarly well adapted to this mode of fishing. Even at the present day the fishermen there shew remarkable skill. They know how to hit upon the exact spot where the fish are hiding, and rarely miss their prey, which they put into a netted bag they wear round their hips, as shewn in my picture.

This peculiar mode of fishing from the shore explains how it was that Jesus was able to speak to the future Apostles on the spot and tell them to follow Him, without having to call to them from afar, and removes a certain amount of the mystery of this scene, described with a brevity so touching.

In the district referred to the mountains gradually become lower, and on some parts of the shore boats can easily approach the land, whilst in others a beach with a gentle slope keeps them at a distance. Here and there, too, small natural harbours are sheltered by blocks of black rock peculiar to these parts, and where this is the case, the population of the shores is considerably denser than elsewhere. It was probably in a comparatively lonely part of the coast that the calling of the Apostles took place. For the rest, however, there is but a narrow tract of land between the beach stretching along the valley of Gennesaret, and the probable site of Capernaum, which was situated on the north of the lake, near the mouth of the Jordan, that is to say near the spot where Bethsaida is supposed to have been. The shores of the lake are, on that side, cut into by five or six small harbours, where the few boats, belonging to the enterprising fishermen who worked off these coasts, could take shelter. Peter and his family, it would appear, were engaged together in a fishing venture.

Calling of Saint James and Saint John

T progressus inde pusillum vidit Jacobum Zebedæi et Joannem fratrem ejus, et ipsos componentes retia in navi.

20. Et statim vocavit illos, et, relicto patre suo Zebedæo in navi cum mercenariis, secuti sunt eum.

S. MARC. — C. I

Calling of Saint James and Saint John.

N D when he had gone a little farther thence, he saw James the son of Zebedee, and John his brother, who also were in the ship mending their nets.

20. And straightway he called them : and they left their father Zebedee in the ship with the hired servants, and went after him.

S. MARK — CH. I

Alphæus was the father of three Apostles : James the Less (meaning the smaller or the younger), Jude, or Thaddæus, and Simon. According to Hegesippus, quoted by Eusebius (II, 23), he was the brother of Saint Joseph, which is why the three disciples, who were the sons of Alphæus, called themselves the brethren of Jesus, this title being the more appropriate to them, in that they were brought up with Him at Nazareth. All the Apostles were of Galilee, Judas Iscariot, the betrayer of the Lord, alone was of Judæa.

Nathanael under the Fig Tree
Saint John – Chap. 1

RAT autem Philippus a Bethsaida, civitate Andreæ et Petri.

45. Invenit Philippus Nathanael, et dicit ei : Quem scripsit Moyses in lege et prophetæ, invenimus, Jesum filium Joseph a Nazareth.

46. Et dixit ei Nathanael : A Nazareth potest aliquid boni esse? Dicit ei Philippus : Veni et vide.

ow Philip was of Bethsaida, the city of Andrew and Peter.

45. Philip findeth Nathanael and saith unto him, We have found him, of whom Moses in the law, and the prophets, did write, Jesus of Nazareth, the son of Joseph.

46. And Nathanael said unto him, Can there any good thing come out of Nazareth? Philip saith unto him, Come and see.

47. Vidit Jesus Nathanael venientem ad se, et dicit de eo : Ecce vere Israelita, in quo dolus non est.

48. Dicit ei Nathanael: Unde me nosti? Respondit Jesus et dixit ei : Priusquam te Philippus vocaret, quum esses sub ficu, vidi te.

49. Respondit ei Nathanael et ait: Rabbi, tu es Filius Dei, tu es rex Israel.

50. Respondit Jesus et dixit ei : Quia dixi tibi : Vidi te sub ficu, credis; majus his videbis.

51. Et dicit ei : Amen amen dico vobis, videbitis cœlum apertum, et angelos Dei ascendentes et descendentes supra Filium hominis.

47. Jesus saw Nathanael coming to him, and saith of him, Behold an Israelite indeed, in whom is no guile!

48. Nathanael saith unto him, Whence knowest thou me? Jesus answered and said unto him, Before that Philip called thee, when thou wast under the fig tree, I saw thee.

49. Nathanael answered and saith unto him, Rabbi, thou art the Son of God; thou art the King of Israel.

50. Jesus answered and saith unto him, Because I said unto thee, I saw thee under the fig tree, believest thou? thou shalt see greater things than these.

51. And he saith unto him, Verily, verily, I say unto you, Hereafter ye shall see heaven open, and the angels of God ascending and descending upon the Son of man.

Saint Bartholomew.   J.-J. T.

The following is the manner in which we have pictured the scene of Nathanael under the fig tree, according to a curious and fairly probable though uncertain interpretation.

The gathering in of the figs takes place in Judæa in the autumn and is celebrated as a fête, much as is the vintage in the south of France. Parties of friends meet beneath the fig trees, and the picking of the fruit serves as a pretext for happy gatherings. Carpets are brought and spread on the ground, and jars full of cooling drinks are provided, for the heat is still considerable, the season being not yet far advanced.

Sometimes the company on these occasions was very mixed, and this, it would appear, was the case with the group frequented by Nathanael.

Now one day, near the road skirting the lake between Magdala and Bethsaida, when he found himself under a fig tree, in a company of doubtful reputation, Nathanael began to be troubled, feeling himself tempted, and on the brink of engaging in an evil course, much like some traveller who takes the wrong path at cross roads. Perhaps this moment was about to influence the whole of his future life and to compromise him for ever, when, all of a sudden, the disciples of the new prophet and the new prophet Himself passed near the group. Nathanael raised his head and, looking up, saw Jesus, His tall figure rising above His followers. The two exchanged a long look, and the expression of the Master was so fraught with mystery, so penetrating, that it touched to the very depths the tempted soul of the other, working in it an instantaneous change.

Then Nathanael, arrested on the edge of what he well knew to be a precipice, felt that he was saved, and he preserved, engraved upon his very heart, the memory of the passing stranger.

Some time passed by, and, when his friends or neighbours spoke to him of the growing reputation of the new prophet, he contented himself with saying, for he did not know Him yet : « Can there any good thing come out of Nazareth?» which was a kind of proverb current in the country, referring to the little town hidden in the mountains and of no reputation.

In old Cairo.

Meanwhile, a fresh incident, as related by the Evangelist, brought Nathanael a second time across the path of Jesus. On the invitation of Philip, this now upright man came to meet Jesus, whom the Apostle had told him was the Messiah, and great was his emotion at recognizing in Him the mysterious passer-by whose mere look had but recently moved him so strangely. He understood now what had taken place within him at the first meeting, the words of the Saviour completed what His look had begun, and Nathanael, transported with joy, exclaimed « Rabbi, Thou art the Son of God. »

The Betrothed of Cana of Galilee
Saint John — Chap. 2

T die tertia nuptiæ factæ sunt in Cana Galilææ, et erat mater Jesu ibi.

2. Vocatus est autem et Jesus et discipuli ejus ad nuptias.

3. Et deficiente vino dicit mater Jesu ad eum : Vinum non habent.

4. Et dicit ei Jesus : Quid mihi et tibi est, mulier? Nondum venit hora mea.

5. Dicit mater ejus ministris : Quodcumque dixerit vobis, facite.

The Betrothed of Cana of Galilee.

ND the third day there was a marriage in Cana of Galilee; and the mother of Jesus was there :

2. And both Jesus was called, and his disciples, to the marriage.

3. And when they wanted wine, the mother of Jesus saith unto him, They have no wine.

4. Jesus saith unto her, Woman, what have I to do with thee? mine hour is not yet come.

5. His mother saith unto the servants, Whatsoever he saith unto you, do it.

The Marriage in Cana
Saint John — Chap. 2

RANT autem ibi lapideæ hydriæ sex positæ secundum purificationem Judæorum, capientes singulæ metretas binas vel ternas.

ND there were set there six waterpots of stone, after the manner of the purifying of the Jews, containing two or three firkins apiece.

THE MARRIAGE IN CANA

7. Dicit eis Jesus : Implete hydrias aqua. Et impleverunt eas usque ad summum.

8. Et dicit eis Jesus : Haurite nunc et ferte architriclino. Et tulerunt.

9. Ut autem gustavit architriclinus aquam vinum factam et non sciebat unde esset (ministri autem sciebant, qui hauserant aquam), vocat sponsum architriclinus,

7. Jesus saith unto them, Fill the waterpots with water. And they filled them up to the brim.

8. And he saith unto them, Draw out now, and bear unto the governor of the feast. And they bare it.

9. When the ruler of the feast had tasted the water that was made wine, and knew not whence it was: (but the servants which drew the water knew;) the governor of the feast called the bridegroom,

The Marriage in Cana.

10. Et dicit ei : Omnis homo primum bonum vinum ponit, et quum inebriati fuerint, tunc id, quod deterius est : tu autem servasti bonum vinum usque adhuc.

11. Hoc fecit initium signorum Jesus in Cana Galilææ, et manifestavit gloriam suam, et crediderunt in eum discipuli ejus.

10. And saith unto him, Every man at the beginning doth set forth good wine; and when men have well drunk, then that which is worse: but thou hast kept the good wine until now.

11. This beginning of miracles did Jesus in Cana of Galilee and manifested forth his glory; and his disciples believed on him.

Jesus went to Cana accompanied by His mother, when He had left Nazareth, having been driven out of that town. This Cana, situated three leagues from Nazareth, and five from Tiberias, was called the little Cana, to distinguish it from the large town of the same name, situated near to Sidon. It was built in a valley full of reeds, and it was to this peculiarity of its site that it owed its name. Not far from it, near the waters of Merom, on the north of the Sea of Tiberias, there was a little lake called the Lake of Crocodiles, the borders of which were also celebrated for the beauty of the reeds growing on them. It was one of these reeds, it is said, which was later given to Our Lord as a sceptre in His Passion.

On His way to Capernaum, then, Jesus passed through Cana, where there was a marriage, to which Jesus, His mother and the disciples accompanying Him, were invited.

According to some accounts, Nathanael, but recently converted and now one of the faithful followers of the Master, was the bridegroom on this occasion, whilst others say he was only the paranymph, or friend of the bridegroom, who was a kind of best man, whose business it was to preside over the wedding ceremonies and feast. It is, moreover, very probable that the man called Nathanael should be identified with the disciple bearing, in the Gospel narrative, the name of Bartholomew, who was one of the twelve Apostles.

Jesus, as will be well understood, had now become of extreme importance in the life of the man under notice, which will explain at once the invitation sent to Him and also the honour with which He and those with Him were received and treated at the wedding.

In fêtes of this description, the repast was served of an evening, the betrothed taking their places beneath a canopy of foliage, or sometimes beneath a kind of trellis-work dome, from which, as shewn in my picture, were suspended all the ornaments that could be collected.

The Talmud enters into the most minute details respecting the marriage ceremony and the customs connected with it, which illustrate well the fastidious character of the observances connected with the civilization of the Jews at this period of their history. It speaks of the powder the women used on various occasions, noting, however, that they refrained from it at the time of Pentecost; alludes to the way in which they darkened the edges of their eyelids with kohl; to the arrangement of their hair beneath their veils; the care with which they removed grey hairs, cut their nails, and scraped away with the aid of a potsherd the down on the lower part of the face. It dwells on the fact that

In old Cairo.

amongst the gifts of the bridegroom to his bride there were always vases of carmine and vermilion, to colour the lips and cheeks and even the nails and palms of the hands, as well as the soles of the feet. Moreover, it gives a description of the toilet, mentioning the bows on the shoulders, which kept the dress in its place, the so-called Tower ornament, the head-dress already referred to, and explained as taking its name from the golden plaques adorning it, on which was a representation of one of the great towns of Palestine, most frequently Jerusalem, in engraving or repoussé work. It even goes so far as to enter into the most minute details about the false hair and the false teeth of the women, explaining that the latter were sometimes made of merely gilded wood. It is careful to tell us that if a wooden tooth should fall out of the mouth on the Sabbath day it was not lawful to pick it up.

All these puerilities, with many others, seemed to the writers of the Talmud to be of very great importance. There was yet another custom which still prevailed at the time of Jesus, to which the Jews clung with the greatest tenacity, as is proved by many a reference to it in the Gospel narrative.

Mary was, it is true, present at the wedding, for the Holy Scriptures tell us so, but she most certainly was not near her divine Son, although most painters take it for granted that she was.

Jewish etiquette did not permit women to sit at table with men, or even to remain in the same room with them during the celebration of a feast. A kind of alcove, or some such recess near at hand, was generally set apart for them, which recess was separated from the rest of the apartment by a grated or openwork partition, through which the women, without being too much in evidence, and whilst still keeping at a distance, could look on and, to a certain extent, take their share in the festivities, hear the various speeches made, admire the elaborate decorations of the guest chamber, and listen to the songs and to the music of the instruments, which added to the bright and festive character of the entertainment.

An Armenian. J.-J. T.

It was probably from some such recess in the background that Mary looked out upon what was going on, and there is little doubt that she seized a moment when Jesus, moving about amongst His fellow guests, passed the partition railing off the Women's corner, to say to Him : « They have no wine. »

The six waterpots of stone referred to in the sacred text were placed there to be used in the purifications so frequent amongst the Jews. The water which they had held had, in fact, been used either for washing the feet and hands before the meal, or for washing dishes and cups during its progress. This will quite easily explain how it was that the water was exhausted at the moment of the intervention of the Master, for the feast was now drawing to its close. Each one of these six waterpots of stone was capable of holding three firkins; and they would have been filled up in the centre of the room in the presence of the guests, for we know that it was in the vacant space, left free of the couches and tables, which were arranged in the form of a horse-shoe, that the servants in attendance stood and waited ready to obey orders. We know what order they received and what happened afterwards.

Ornament in gilded metal, from the Es-Sakhra Mosque. J.-J. T.

Jesus goes up to Jerusalem
Saint John – Chap. 2

ost hoc descendit Capharnaum, ipse et mater ejus et fratres ejus et discipuli ejus, et ibi manserunt non multis diebus.

13. Et prope erat pascha Judæorum, et ascendit Jesus Jerosolymam.

fter this he went down to Capernaum, he, and his mother, and his brethren, and his disciples: and they continued there not many days.

13. And the Jews' passover was at hand, and Jesus went up to Jerusalem.

Interview between Jesus and Nicodemus
Saint John — Chap. 3

RAT autem homo ex Pharisæis, Nicodemus nomine, princeps Judæorum.
2. Hic venit ad Jesum nocte et dixit ei : Rabbi, scimus quia a Deo venisti magister; nemo enim potest hæc signa facere, quæ tu facis, nisi fuerit Deus cum eo.

3. Respondit Jesus et dixit ei : Amen amen dico tibi, nisi quis renatus fuerit denuo, non potest videre regnum Dei.

4. Dicit ad eum Nicodemus : Quomodo potest homo nasci, quum sit senex? numquid potest in ventrem matris suæ iterato introire et renasci?

5. Respondit Jesus : Amen amen dico tibi, nisi quis renatus fuerit ex aqua

HERE was a man of the Pharisees, named Nicodemus, a ruler of the Jews:
2. The same came to Jesus by night, and said unto him, Rabbi, we know that thou art a teacher come from God : for no man can do these miracles that thou doest, except God be with him.

3. Jesus answered and said unto him, Verily, verily, I say unto thee, Except a man be born again, he cannot see the kingdom of God.

4. Nicodemus saith unto him, How can a man be born when he is old? can he enter the second time into his mother's womb, and be born?

5. Jesus answered, Verily, verily, I say unto thee, Except a man be born of

Interview between Jesus and Nicodemus. — J.-J. T.

et Spiritu sancto, non potest introire in regnum Dei.

6. Quod natum est ex carne, caro est, et quod natum est ex Spiritu, spiritus est.

7. Non mireris quia dixi tibi : Oportet vos nasci denuo.

8. Spiritus ubi vult spirat, et vocem ejus audis, sed nescis, unde veniat aut quo vadat : sic est omnis, qui natus est ex Spiritu.

9. Respondit Nicodemus et dixit ei : Quomodo possunt hæc fieri?

10. Respondit Jesus et dixit ei : Tu es magister in Israel, et hæc ignoras?

11. Amen amen dico tibi, quia quod scimus loquimur, et quod vidimus testamur, et testimonium nostrum non accipitis.

12. Si terrena dixi vobis et non creditis, quomodo, si dixero vobis cœlestia, credetis?

13. Et nemo ascendit in cœlum, nisi qui descendit de cœlo, Filius hominis, qui est in cœlo.

14. Et sicut Moyses exaltavit serpentem in deserto, ita exaltari oportet Filium hominis,

15. Ut omnis, qui credit in ipsum, non pereat, sed habeat vitam æternam.

16. Sic enim Deus dilexit mundum, ut Filium suum unigenitum daret, ut

water and of the Spirit, he cannot enter into the kingdom of God.

6. That which is born of the flesh is flesh; and that which is born of the Spirit is spirit.

7. Marvel not that I said unto thee, Ye must be born again.

8. The wind bloweth where it listeth, and thou hearest the sound thereof, but canst not tell whence it cometh, and whither it goeth : so is every one that is born of the Spirit.

9. Nicodemus answered and said unto him, How can these things be?

10. Jesus answered and said unto him, Art thou a master of Israel, and knowest not these things?

11. Verily, verily, I say unto thee, We speak that we do know, and testify that we have seen; and ye receive not our witness.

12. If I have told you earthly things, and ye believe not, how shall ye believe, if I tell you of heavenly things?

13. And no man hath ascended up to heaven, but he that came down from heaven, even the Son of man which is in heaven.

14. And as Moses lifted up the serpent in the wilderness, even so must the Son of man be lifted up :

15. That whosoever believeth in him should not perish, but have eternal life.

16. For God so loved the world, that he gave his only begotten Son that

Nicodemus

omnis, qui credit in eum, non pereat, sed habeat vitam æternam.

17. Non enim misit Deus Filium suum in mundum, ut judicet mundum, sed ut salvetur mundus per ipsum.

18. Qui credit in eum, non judicatur, qui autem non credit, jam judicatus est, quia non credit in nomine unigeniti Filii Dei.

whosoever believeth in him should not perish, but have everlasting life.

17. For God sent not his Son into the world to condemn the world ; but that the world through him might be saved.

18. He that believeth on him is not condemned : but he that believeth not is condemned already, because he hath not believed in the name of the only begotten Son of God.

In the Island of Rhoda, Old Cairo.

The Rabbis tell us that the Hebrew name of Nicodemus the disciple of Jesus, was Bonoi Ben Gorion. He was a priest and a member of the Sanhedrim, or Supreme Council of the Jewish people. His wealth was considerable and his influence very great. It is even said that he was superintendent of the water supply of Jerusalem, and it is to him the story refers telling how, every time he went to the Temple, he had a fresh carpet spread out for him, giving the old ones to the poor, and never using the same one twice. Nicodemus was by no means what we should call at the present day a parvenu; he was of a very ancient and illustrious race; his family originally came from Jericho, and he himself was a disciple of the celebrated Hillel, who had founded in his own house an academy and school which had become famous.

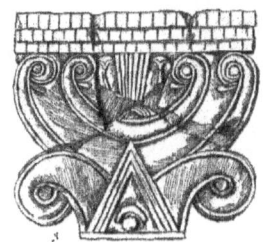

The disciples of Jesus baptizing
Saint John – Chap. 4

 T ergo cognovit Jesus, quia audierunt Pharisæi, quod Jesus plures discipulos facit et baptizat quam Joannes,

2. Quamquam Jesus non baptizaret, sed discipuli ejus,

3. Reliquit Judæam et abiit iterum in Galilæam.

4. Oportebat autem eum transire per Samariam.

 HEN therefore the Lord knew how the Pharisees had heard that Jesus made and baptized more disciples than John,

2. Though Jesus himself baptized not, but his disciples,

3. He left Judæa, and departed again into Galilee.

4. And he must needs go through Samaria.

The Man with an infirmity of thirty and eight years
Saint John — Chap. 5

post hæc erat dies festus Judæorum, et ascendit Jesus Jerosolymis. 2. Est autem Jerosolymis probatica piscina, quæ cognominatur hebraice Bethsaida, quinque porticus habens.

3. In his jacebat multitudo magna languentium, cæcorum, claudorum, aridorum, exspectantium aquæ motum.

4. Angelus autem Domini descendebat secundum tempus in piscinam, et movebatur aqua. Et qui prior descendisset in piscinam post motionem aquæ, sanus fiebat a quacumque detinebatur infirmitate.

5. Erat autem quidam homo ibi, triginta et octo annos habens in infirmitate sua.
6. Hunc quum vidisset Jesus jacen-

after this there was a feast of the Jews; and Jesus went up to Jerusalem. 2. Now there is at Jerusalem by the sheep market a pool, which is called in the Hebrew tongue Bethesda, having five porches.

3. In these lay a great multitude of impotent folk, of blind, halt, withered, waiting for the moving of the water.

4. For an angel went down at a certain season into the pool, and troubled the water: whosoever then first after the troubling of the water stepped in was made whole of whatsoever disease he had.

5. And a certain man was there, which had an infirmity thirty and eight years.
6. When Jesus saw him lie, and knew

tem, et cognovisset quia jam multum tempus haberet, dicit ei : Vis sanus fieri?

7. Respondit ei languidus : Domine, hominem non habeo, ut, quum turbata fuerit aqua, mittat me in piscinam ; dum venio enim ego, alius ante me descendit.

8. Dicit ei Jesus : Surge, tolle grabatum tuum et ambula.

9. Et statim sanus factus est homo ille, et sustulit grabatum suum et ambulabat. Erat autem sabbatum in die illo.

10. Dicebant ergo Judæi illi, qui sanatus fuerat : Sabbatum est, non licet tibi tollere grabatum tuum.

11. Respondit eis : Qui me sanum fecit, ille mihi dixit : Tolle grabatum tuum et ambula.

12. Interrogaverunt ergo eum : Quis est ille homo, qui dixit tibi : Tolle grabatum tuum et ambula?

13. Is autem, qui sanus fuerat effectus, nesciebat quis esset. Jesus enim declinavit a turba constituta in loco.

14. Postea invenit eum Jesus in templo et dixit illi : Ecce sanus factus es ; jam noli peccare, ne deterius tibi aliquid contingat.

that he had been now a long time in that case, he saith unto him, Wilt thou be made whole ?

7. The impotent man answered him, Sir, I have no man, when the water is troubled, to put me into the pool : but while I am coming, another steppeth down before me.

8. Jesus saith unto him, Rise, take up thy bed, and walk.

9. And immediately the man was made whole, and took up his bed, and walked : and on the same day was the sabbath.

10. The Jews therefore said unto him that was cured, It is the sabbath day : it is not lawful for thee to carry thy bed.

11. He answered them, He that made me whole, the same said unto me, Take up thy bed, and walk.

12. Then asked they him, What man is that which said unto thee, Take up thy bed, and walk ?

13. And he that was healed wist not who it was : for Jesus had conveyed himself away, a multitude being in that place.

14. Afterward Jesus findeth him in the temple, and said unto him, Behold, thou art made whole : sin no more, lest a worse thing come unto thee.

A typical woman of Jerusalem. J.-J. T.

15. Abiit ille homo et nuntiavit Judæis, quia Jesus esset, qui fecit eum sanum.

15. The man departed and told the Jews that it was Jesus which had made him whole.

The Piscina Probatica or Pool of Bethesda
Saint John — Chap. 5

NGELUS autem Domini descendebat secundum tempus in piscinam, et movebatur aqua. Et qui prior descendisset in piscinam post motionem aquæ, sanus fiebat a quacumque detinebatur infirmitate.

OR an angel went down at a certain season into the pool, and troubled the water; whosoever then first after the troubling of the water stepped in was made whole of whatsoever disease he had.

The site of this pool is very doubtful. Traces of it are supposed to have been found near the Church of Saint Anne, where excavations have brought to light the remains of a chapel dating from the time of the Crusades. There is, however, nothing to prove the attempted identification, and we should, perhaps, be more justified in supposing that the « pool which was troubled » was situated on the south of the Temple, in the so-called Ophel suburb. According to some interpreters, in fact, the word Bethesda signifies « the house of the waterfall » or « the place of the flowing of water », a name having reference to the flowing of the water from the Temple reservoirs, which would place the pool on the south rather than on the north.

The Priests used this water in the Temple for various purposes. It is said to have acted as a purgative, and to have been of service in cases of gout, rheumatism, paralysis and consumption. When the air bubbles were rising to the surface, and the water was lukewarm, sufferers plunged into it with all possible speed.

It is related that, a short time after the death of Jesus, Herod wished to enlarge this pool and widen the channels and reservoirs; but the spring which fed it suddenly dried up, and water did not flow from it again, till everything was restored to its original condition.

Saint Jerome and Eusebius both testify that in their day a kind of double reservoir was still shewn at Jerusalem, one pool of which was filled by the periodical rains, whilst the other contained water of a perfectly red colour, as if, it was said, it still retained the hue given to it by the blood of the victims sacrificed in past days.

For the rest, in addition to this « Piscina Probatica », which was used for special purposes, the system of the water supply of Jerusalem was extremely well organized. On the west, at the top of the valley of Gihon, was the Birket Mamilla; lower down, the cistern now called the Birket el Sultan; then again, near to Mount Calvary, the amygdalum or Pool of Hezekiah. On the east is yet another pool, called that of the rams, which was used in the service of the Temple; whilst, on the south of the town, was the so-called Fountain of the Holy Virgin, and the Pool of Siloam.

Moreover, every house had its cistern intended for the reception of rainwater, and wherever the nature of the surface of the ground permitted the accumulation of water, in the courts and porches of houses, in open places, and at cross-roads, for instance, similar reservoirs were dug out, so that plenty of water was always secured for ordinary domestic purposes.

The chief sources of supply of the town of Jerusalem, however, were the reservoirs, now known as Solomon's pools, excavated in the rock near Etham, from which great quantities of water, following the natural slope of the mountain, flowed by way of that town and Bethlehem, accumulating in the Temple reservoirs, and, with the cisterns which supplied the numerous porches, amply sufficing for every requirement.

The aqueduct through which the water flowed emptied its contents into three huge basins constructed, it is said, by Solomon, but it seems more probable that they were the work of the Canaanites and that the great king did no more than restore them, though his so doing at once led to their being called by his name.

The three basins to which we are now referring were fed by the spring called the « Sealed Fountain » (fons signatus), alluded to in the Song of Solomon (Chap. IV, verse 12). Lastly, the purest water in Jerusalem, which for this reason was always used for making the unleavened bread for the Passover, was that of the well now known as the Aïn siti Mariam, and spoken of in the Bible as El Rogel. According to tradition, it was near this well that the scene occurred on the eve of the Passion, when Peter and John met the man bearing a pitcher of water (Saint Luke, XXII, verse 10).

The Piscina Probatica.

The Woman of Samaria at the Well
Saint John — Chap. 4

PORTEBAT autem eum transire per Samariam.
5. Venit ergo in civitatem Samariæ, quæ dicitur Sichar, juxta prædium, quod dedit Jacob Joseph filio suo.

6. Erat autem ibi fons Jacob. Jesus ergo fatigatus ex itinere sedebat sic supra fontem ; hora erat quasi sexta.

AND he must needs go through Samaria.
5. Then cometh he to a city of Samaria, which is called Sychar, near to the parcel of ground that Jacob gave to his son Joseph.

6. Now Jacob's well was there. Jesus therefore, being wearied with his journey, sat thus on the well : and it was about the sixth hour.

7. Venit mulier de Samaria haurire aquam. Dicit ei Jesus : Da mihi bibere.

8. Discipuli enim ejus abierant in civitatem, ut cibos emerent.

9. Dicit ergo ei mulier illa Samaritana : Quomodo tu, Judæus quum sis, bibere a me poscis, quæ sum mulier Samaritana? Non enim coutuntur Judæi Samaritanis.

10. Respondit Jesus et dixit ei : Si scires donum Dei et quis est, qui dicit tibi : Da mihi bibere : tu forsitan petisses ab eo, et dedisset tibi aquam vivam.

11. Dicit ei mulier : Domine, neque in quo haurias habes, et puteus altus est; unde ergo habes aquam vivam?

12. Numquid tu major es patre nostro Jacob, qui dedit nobis puteum, et ipse ex eo bibit, et filii ejus, et pecora ejus?

13. Respondit Jesus et dixit ei : Omnis, qui bibit ex aqua hac, sitiet iterum ; qui autem biberit ex aqua, quam ego dabo ei, non sitiet in æternum ;

14. Sed aqua, quam ego dabo ei, fiet in eo fons aquæ salientis in vitam æternam.

Saint Philip.   J.-J. T.

7. There cometh a woman of Samaria to draw water : Jesus saith unto her, Give me to drink.

8. For his disciples were gone away unto the city to buy meat.

9. Then saith the woman of Samaria unto him, How is it that thou, being a Jew, askest drink of me, which am a woman of Samaria ? for the Jews have no dealings with the Samaritans.

10. Jesus answered and said unto her, If thou knewest the gift of God, and who it is that saith to thee, Give me to drink; thou wouldest have asked of him and he would have given thee living water.

11. The woman saith unto him, Sir, thou hast nothing to draw with, and the well is deep : from whence then hast thou that living water?

12. Art thou greater than our father Jacob, which gave us the well, and drank thereof himself, and his children, and his cattle?

13. Jesus answered and said unto her, Whosoever drinketh of this water shall thirst again :

14. But whosoever drinketh of the water that I shall give him shall never thirst; but the water that I shall give him shall be in him a well of water springing up into everlasting life.

15. Dicit ad eum mulier: Domine, da mihi hanc aquam, ut non sitiam neque veniam huc haurire.

15. The woman saith unto him, Sir, give me this water, that I thirst not neither come hither to draw.

Jesus in the Synagogue
Saint Luke — Chap. 4

T venit Nazareth, ubi erat nutritus, et intravit secundum consuetudinem suam die sabbati in synagogam, et surrexit legere.

17. Et traditus est illi liber Isaiæ prophetæ. Et ut revolvit librum, invenit locum ubi scriptum erat:

18. Spiritus Domini super me: propter quod unxit me, evangelizare pauperibus misit me, sanare contritos corde,

ND he came to Nazareth, where he had been brought up: and, as his custom was, he went into the synagogue on the sabbath day, and stood up for to read.

17. And there was delivered unto him the book of the prophet Esaias. And when he had opened the book, he found the place where it was written,

18. The Spirit of the Lord is upon me, because he hath anointed me to preach the gospel to the poor; he hath sent me to heal the broken hearted, to preach deliverance to the captives, and recovering of sight to the blind, to set at liberty them that are bruised,

A Synagogue in Jerusalem.

19. Prædicare captivis remissionem et cæcis visum, dimittere confractos in remissionem, prædicare annum Domini acceptum, et diem retributionis.

19. To preach the acceptable year of the Lord.

THE MINISTRY

20. Et quum plicuisset librum, reddidit ministro et sedit, et omnium in synagoga oculi erant intendentes in eum.

21. Cœpit autem dicere ad illos: Quia hodie impleta est hæc scriptura in auribus vestris.

22. Et omnes testimonium illi dabant, et mirabantur in verbis gratiæ, quæ procedebant de ore ipsius, et dicebant: Nonne hic est filius Joseph?

23. Et ait illis: Utique dicetis mihi hanc similitudinem: Medice, cura te ipsum ; quanta audivimus facta in Capharnaum, fac et hic in patria tua.

24. Ait autem: Amen dico vobis, quia nemo propheta acceptus est in patria sua.

20. And he closed the book, and he gave it again to the minister, and sat down. And the eyes of all them that were in the synagogue were fastened on him.

21. And he began to say unto them, This day is this scripture fulfilled in your ears.

22. And all bare him witness, and wondered at the gracious words which proceeded out of his mouth. And they said, Is not this Joseph's son?

23. And he said unto them, Ye will surely say unto me this proverb, Physician, heal thyself: whatsoever we have heard done in Capernaum, do also here in thy country.

24. And he said, Verily I say unto you, No prophet is accepted in his own country.

Jesus in the Synagogue.   J. J. T.

Every respectable male member of the community might be requested to explain the Bible. In fact, this task might be performed by any one who had reached the age of 13 years.

When some Rabbi or foreign doctor happened to be present in the Synagogue, it was the custom to pay him the compliment of asking him to comment upon the Holy Scriptures. This, no doubt, often occurred in the case of Our Lord and Saviour Jesus Christ. We know, from the account given in the Acts of the Apostles, that later, Saint Paul, in his Missionary journeys, turned this custom to account, to make his way into the Jewish Synagogues and there bear witness to Jesus.

The Brow of the Hill near Nazareth
Saint Luke — Chap. 4

IN veritate dico vobis, multæ viduæ erant in diebus Eliæ in Israel, quando clausum est cœlum annis tribus et mensibus sex, quum facta esset fames magna in omni terra:

26. Et ad nullam illarum missus est Elias, nisi in Sarepta Sidoniæ ad mulierem viduam.

27. Et multi leprosi erant in Israel sub Elisæo propheta, et nemo eorum mundatus est, nisi Naaman Syrus.

28. Et repleti sunt omnes in synagoga ira hæc audientes.

29. Et surrexerunt et ejecerunt illum extra civitatem, et duxerunt illum usque ad supercilium montis, super quem civitas illorum erat ædificata, ut præcipitarent eum.

30. Ipse autem transiens per medium illorum ibat.

UT I tell you of a truth, many widows were in Israel in the days of Elias, when the heaven was shut up three years and six months, when great famine was throughout all the land;

26. But unto none of them was Elias sent, save unto Sarepta, a city of Sidon, unto a woman that was a widow.

27. And many lepers were in Israel in the time of Eliseus the prophet; and none of them was cleansed, saving Naaman the Syrian.

28. And all they in the synagogue, when they heard these things, were filled with wrath.

29. And rose up, and thrust him out of the city, and led him unto the brow of the hill whereon their city was built, that they might cast him down headlong.

30. But he passing through the midst of them went his way.

The Brow of the Hill near Nazareth.

The Hidden Treasure

Saint Matthew — Chap. 13

UNC justi fulgebunt sicut sol in regno Patris eorum. Qui habet aures audiendi, audiat.

HEN shall the righteous shine forth as the sun in the kingdom of their Father. Who hath ears to hear, let him hear.

The Hidden Treasure.

44. Simile est regnum cœlorum thesauro abscondito in agro, quem qui invenit homo abscondit, et præ gaudio illius vadit, et vendit universa quæ habet, et emit agrum illum.

44. Again, the kingdom of heaven is like unto treasure hid in a field; the which when a man hath found, he hideth, and for joy thereof goeth and selleth all that he hath, and buyeth that field.

The Man at the Plough

Saint Luke — Chap. 9

IXITQUE ei Jesus : Sine ut mortui sepeliant mortuos suos; tu autem vade et annuntia regnum Dei.

61. Et ait alter : Sequar te, Domine, sed permitte mihi primum renuntiare his, quæ domi sunt.

62. Ait ad illum Jesus: Nemo mittens

ESUS said unto him, Let the dead bury their dead: but go thou and preach the kingdom of God.

61. And another also said, Lord, I will follow thee; but let me first go bid them farewell, which are at home at my house.

62. And Jesus said unto him, No man,

manum suam ad aratrum et respiciens retro, aptus est regno Dei.

The Man at the Plough.

having put his hand to the plough, and looking back, is fit for the kingdom of God.

The husbandman represented in our engraving is doubly in fault. He is not only « looking back, having put his hand to the plough », and as a result deviating from his furrows, but he is sinning against an ordinance of the Jewish law, which says : « Thou shalt not plow with an ox and an ass together ». Deut. XXII, verse 10. This rule, with many similar ones to be met with in the Bible, appears to have been laid down with a view to inculcating in the minds of the Hebrews feelings of humanity, even for the brute beasts, and against this rule no doubt many rebelled.

In a passage in the second Epistle to the Corinthians, Chap. VI, verse 14, Saint Paul applies the passage quoted above to the relations between the Christians and the Gentiles : « Be ye not unequally yoked together with unbelievers : for what fellowship hath righteousness with unrighteousness ? »

The Man with an unclean Spirit in the Synagogue
Saint Mark — Chap. 1

T ingrediuntur Capharnaum, et statim sabbatis ingressus in synagogam docebat eos.

22. Et stupebant super doctrina ejus; erat enim docens eos quasi potestatem habens, et non sicut scribæ.

23. Et erat in synagoga eorum homo

ND they went into Capernaum; and straightway on the sabbath day he entered into the synagogue, and taught.

22. And they were astonished at his doctrine : for he taught them as one that had authority, and not as the scribes.

23. And there was in their synagogue

in spiritu immundo, et exclamavit,

24. Dicens: Quid nobis et tibi, Jesu Nazarene? venisti perdere nos? scio qui sis, Sanctus Dei.

25. Et comminatus est ei Jesus, dicens: Obmutesce, et exi de homine.

26. Et discerpens eum spiritus immundus et reclamans voce magna exiit ab eo.

27. Et mirati sunt omnes, ita ut conquirent inter se dicentes: Quidnam est hoc? quænam doctrina hæc nova? quia in potestate etiam spiritibus immundis imperat, et obediunt ei.

28. Et processit rumor ejus statim in omnem regionem Galilææ.

a man with an unclean spirit; and he cried out,

24. Saying, Let us alone; what have we to do with thee, thou Jesus of Nazareth? art thou come to destroy us? I know thee who thou art, the Holy One of God.

25. And Jesus rebuked him, saying, Hold thy peace, and come out of him.

26. And when the unclean spirit had torn him, and cried with a loud voice, he came out of him.

27. And they were all amazed, insomuch that they questioned among themselves, saying, What thing is this? what new doctrine is this? for with authority commandeth he even the unclean spirits, and they do obey him.

28. And immediately his fame spread abroad throughout all the region round about Galilee.

Healing of Simon's wife's mother
Saint Mark — Chap. 1

T protinus egredientes de synagoga venerunt in domum Simonis et Andreæ cum Jacobo et Joanne.

30. Decumbebat autem socrus Simonis febricitans, et statim dicunt ei de illa.

31. Et accedens elevavit eam apprehensa manu ejus, et continuo dimisit febris, et ministrabat eis.

ND forthwith, when they were come out of the synagogue, they entered into the house of Simon and Andrew, with James and John.

30. But Simon's wife's mother lay sick of a fever, and anon they tell him of her.

31. And he came and took her by the hand, and lifted her up; and immediately the fever left her, and she ministered unto them.

All the city was gathered together
Saint Mark — Chap. 1

ESPERE autem facto quum occidisset sol, afferebant ad eum omnes male habentes et dæmonia habentes.

33. Et erat omnis civitas congregata ad januam.
34. Et curavit multos, qui vexabantur variis languoribus, et dæmonia multa ejiciebat, et non sinebat ea loqui, quoniam sciebant eum.

ND at even, when the sun did set, they brought unto him all that were diseased, and them that were possessed with devils.

33. And all the city was gathered together at the door.
34. And he healed many that were sick of divers diseases, and cast out many devils; and suffered not the devils to speak, because they knew him.

Saint Simon. J.-J. T.

The streets of towns in the East, especially those of Galilee and Judæa, are very narrow and tortuous. They are, moreover, very dark, on account of the way in which most of them are shut in by the arches supporting the houses. These arches, which connect the houses on either side together, add greatly to their solidity, so that when the modern ædile, with a view to letting in more light, orders their removal, recourse has to be had to props, to prevent the buildings from falling down.

It is several times stated in the Gospels that when Jesus drove out evil spirits, they bore witness to Him and acknowledged His superhuman power. In the case under notice, Jesus rebuked the unclean spirit, saying, « Hold thy peace », because that spirit had cried out, « I know thee who thou art », that is to say, he guessed the divine character of Christ, and His mission as the Messiah, from His works. Now it did not suit Our Lord to reveal before His hour was come a truth so transcendent, and one for which men, especially His fellow countrymen, were so little prepared. It was outside the house of Simon that the scene described by Saint Mark took place.

ALL THE CITY WAS GATHERED TOGETHER AT THE DOOR

MrpU

The Man who laid up Treasure
Saint Luke — Chap. 12

IXIT autem similitudinem ad illos dicens : Hominis cujusdam divitis uberes fructus ager attulit. 17. Et cogitabat intra se dicens : Quid faciam ? quia non habeo quo congregem fructus meos.

18. Et dixit : Hoc faciam : destruam horrea mea, et majora faciam, et illuc congregabo omnia, quæ nata sunt mihi et bona mea.

19. Et dicam animæ meæ : Anima, habes multa bona posita in annos plurimos; requiesce, comede, bibe, epulare.

20. Dixit autem illi Deus : Stulte, hac nocte animam tuam repetunt a te; quæ autem parasti, cujus erunt?

21. Sic est qui sibi thesaurizat, et non est in Deum dives.

ND he spake a parable unto them, saying, The ground of a certain rich man brought forth plentifully : 17. And he thought within himself, saying, What shall I do, because I have no room where to bestow my fruits?

18. And he said, This will I do : I will pull down my barns, and build greater; and there will I bestow all my fruits and my goods.

19. And I will say to my soul, Soul, thou hast much goods laid up for many years; take thine ease, eat, drink, *and* be merry.

20. But God said unto him, *Thou* fool, this night thy soul shall be required of thee : then whose shall those things be, which thou hast provided?

21. So *is* he that layeth up treasure for himself, and is not rich toward God.

The man who laid up treasure.   J.-J. T.

Jesus went out into a desert place
Saint Luke – Chap. 4

ACTA autem die egressus ibat in desertum locum, et turbæ requirebant eum, et venerunt usque ad ipsum, et detinebant illum, ne discederet ab eis.

43. Quibus ille ait : Quia et aliis civitatibus oportet me evangelizare regnum Dei, quia ideo missus sum.

ND when it was day, he departed and went into a desert place : and the people sought him, and came unto him, and stayed him, that he should not depart from them.

43. And he said unto them, I must preach the kingdom of God to other cities also : for therefore am I sent.

Jesus teaching in the Synagogue
Saint Matthew — Chap. 4

T circuibat Jesus totam Galilæam, docens in synagogis eorum, et prædicans evangelium regni, et sanans omnem languorem et omnem infirmitatem in populo.

24. Et abiit opinio ejus in totam Syriam, et obtulerunt ei omnes male habentes, variis languoribus et tormentis comprehensos, et qui dæmonia habebant, et lunaticos et paralyticos, et curavit eos.

25. Et secutæ sunt eum turbæ multæ de Galilæa et Decapoli et de Jerosolymis et de Judæa et de trans Jordanem.

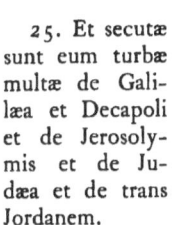

ND Jesus went about all Galilee, teaching in their synagogues, and preaching the gospel of the kingdom, and healing all manner of sickness and all manner of disease among the people.

24. And his fame went throughout all Syria : and they brought unto him all sick people that were taken with divers diseases and torments, and those which were possessed with devils, and those which were lunatick, and those that had the palsy; and he healed them.

25. And there followed him great multitudes of people from Galilee, and *from* Decapolis, and *from* Jerusalem, and *from* Judæa, and *from* beyond Jordan.

The vine dresser and the fig-tree
Saint Luke – Chap. 13

ICEBAT autem et hanc similitudinem : Arborem fici habebat quidam plantatam in vinea sua, et venit quærens fructum in illa, et non invenit.

7. Dixit autem ad cultorem vineæ : Ecce anni tres sunt, ex quo venio quærens fructum in ficulnea hac, et non invenio; succide ergo illam : ut quid etiam terram occupat ?

8. At ille respondens dicit illi : Domine, dimitte illam et hoc anno, usque dum fodiam circa illam et mittam stercora,

9. Et siquidem fecerit fructum ; sin autem, in futurum succides eam.

E spake also this parable : A certain *man* had a fig-tree planted in his vineyard; and he came and sought fruit thereon, and found none.

7. Then said he unto the dresser of his vineyard : Behold, these three years I come seeking fruit on this fig-tree, and find none : cut it down ; why cumbereth it the ground ?

8. And he answering said unto him : Lord, let it alone this year also, till I shall dig about it, and dung *it :*

9. And if it bear fruit, *well;* and if not, *then* after that thou shalt cut it down.

The vine dresser and the fig-tree. J. J. T.

In a melancholy, deserted spot at the bottom of some ravine, languished a ricketty old fig-tree, growing from the stony soil. Its uselessness condemned it to the fire, just as that of the Jews, symbolized in the parable, condemned them to dispersion. The dresser or gardener of the vineyard, who represents Christ, intercedes for the last time with the Lord of the vineyard, saying : « Let it alone this year also. »

The healing of the Ruler's son
Saint John — Chap. 4

ENIT ergo iterum in Cana Galilæa, ubi fecit aquam vinum. Et erat quidam regulus, cujus filius infirmabatur Capharnaum.

47. Hic quum audisset, quia Jesus adveniret a Judæa in Galilæam, abiit ad eum et rogabat eum, ut descenderet et sanaret filium ejus; incipiebat enim mori.

48. Dixit ergo Jesus ad eum : Nisi signa et prodigia videritis, non creditis.

49. Dicit ad eum regulus : Domine, descende prius quam moriatur filius meus.

50. Dicit ei Jesus : Vade, filius tuus vivit. Credidit homo sermoni, quem dixit ei Jesus, et ibat.

51. Jam autem eo descendente servi occurrerunt ei et nuntiaverunt dicentes, quia filius ejus viveret.

52. Interrogabat ergo horam ab eis, in qua melius habuerit. Et dixerunt ei : Quia heri hora septima reliquit eum febris.

o Jesus came again into Cana of Galilee, where he made the water wine. And there was a certain nobleman, whose son was sick at Capernaum.

47. When he heard that Jesus was come out of Judæa into Galilee, he went unto him, and besought him that he would come down, and heal his son : for he was at the point of death.

48. Then said Jesus unto him, Except ye see signs and wonders, ye will not believe.

49. The nobleman saith unto him, Sir, come down ere my child die.

50. Jesus saith unto him, Go thy way; thy son liveth. And the man believed the word that Jesus had spoken unto him, and he went his way.

51. And as he was now going down, his servants met him, and told *him*, saying, Thy son liveth.

52. Then enquired he of them the hour when he began to amend. And they said unto him, Yesterday at the seventh hour the fever left him.

Saint Paul. J.-J. T.

THE MINISTRY

The healing of the Ruler's son.

53. Cognovit ergo pater, quia illa hora erat, in qua dixit ei Jesus : Filius tuus vivit; et credidit ipse et domus ejus tota.
54. Hoc iterum secundum signum fecit Jesus, quum venisset a Judæa in Galilæam.

53. So the father knew that *it was* at the same hour, in the which Jesus said unto him, Thy son liveth : and himself believed, and his whole house.
54. This *is* again the second miracle *that* Jesus did, when he was come out of Judæa into Galilee.

In Dr Sepp's « Life of Our Lord and Saviour Jesus Christ », to which I am indebted for many interesting details, he says that the name of the ruler referred to in the sacred text (whom he confuses with the centurion, who said « Domine, non sum dignus », etc.) was Chuza. Truth to tell, we have very little definite information as to the ruler's identity, but, fortunately, an ancient Idumean family register has come down to us, in which we find the name of Chuza side by side with that of Herod. From the moment of this miracle we find Johanna, the wife of the officer named Chuza, amongst the followers of Jesus.

Jesus preaching in a ship.

Jesus preaching in a ship
Saint Mark — Chap. 4

T iterum cœpit docere ad mare, et congregata est ad eum turba multa, ita ut navim ascendens sederet in mari, et omnis turba circa mare super terram erat.

2. Et docebat eos in parabolis multa.

ND he began again to teach by the sea side: and there was gathered unto him a great multitude, so that he entered into a ship, and sat in the sea; and the whole multitude was by the sea on the land.

2. And he taught them many things by parables.

The first Miraculous Draught of Fishes
Saint Luke – Chap. 5

ACTUM est autem, quum turbæ irruerent in eum, ut audirent verbum Dei, et ipse stabat secus stagnum Genesareth.

2. Et vidit duas naves stantes secus stagnum; piscatores autem descenderant et lavabant retia.

3. Ascendens autem in unam navim, quæ erat Simonis, rogavit eum a terra reducere pusillum. Et sedens docebat de navicula turbas.

4. Ut cessavit autem loqui, dixit ad Simonem : Duc in altum et laxate retia vestra in capturam.

5. Et respondens Simon dixit illi : Præceptor, per totam noctem laborantes nihil cepimus; in verbo autem tuo laxabo rete.

6. Et quum hoc fecissent, concluserunt piscium multitudinem copiosam; rumpebatur autem rete eorum.

7. Et annuerunt sociis, qui erant in alia navi, ut venirent et adjuvarent eos.

ND it came to pass, that, as the people pressed upon him to hear the word of God, he stood by the lake of Gennesaret,

2. And saw two ships standing by the lake : but the fishermen were gone out of them, and were washing *their* nets.

3. And he entered into one of the ships, which was Simon's, and prayed him that he would thrust out a little from the land. And he sat down, and taught the people out of the ship.

A corner in the Valley of Hinnom.

4. Now when he had left speaking, he said unto Simon, Launch out into the deep, and let down your nets for a draught.

5. And Simon answering said unto him, Master, we have toiled all the night, and have taken nothing: nevertheless at thy word I will let down the net.

6. And when they had this done, they inclosed a great multitude of fishes : and their net brake.

7. And they beckoned unto *their* partners, which were in the other ship,

THE FIRST MIRACULOUS DRAUGHT OF FISHES

Et venerunt et impleverunt ambas naviculas, ita ut pæne mergerentur.

8. Quod quum videret Simon Petrus, procidit ad genua Jesu dicens : Exi a me, quia homo peccator sum, Domine.

9. Stupor enim circumdederat eum, et omnes, qui cum illo erant in captura piscium, quam ceperant;

10. Similiter autem Jacobum et Joannem, filios Zebedæi, qui erant socii Simonis. Et ait ad Simonem Jesus : Noli timere; ex hoc jam homines eris capiens.

11. Et subductis ad terram navibus, relictis omnibus secuti sunt eum.

At the time of Jesus Christ, the Lake of Tiberias was much frequented, but now it is entirely deserted. At the time of my visit to it, about 1888, there were not more than fifteen boats to be seen on it, and Lamartine tells us he did not see one, a great change from the time of the historian Josephus, who speaks of four thousand boats, such as skiffs, barges and other craft of various build, with more important vessels. Not only were there then upon the lake the fleets of the various fishing communities which were dotted along the

that they should come and help them. And they came, and filled both the ships, so that they began to sink.

8. When Simon Peter saw *it*, he fell down at Jesus' knees, saying, Depart from me ; for I am a sinful man, O Lord.

9. For he was astonished, and all that were with him, at the draught of the fishes which they had taken :

10. And so *was* also James, and John, the sons of Zebedee, which were partners with Simon. And Jesus said unto Simon, Fear not; from henceforth thou shalt catch men.

11. And when they had brought their ships to land, they forsook all, and followed him.

Saint James the Greater.   J.-J. T.

coast, but there were also the ferry boats, used for taking passengers for different kinds of merchandise to and fro between the shores, as well as the craft belonging to the garrison of the town of Tiberias, then a regular military station.

Josephus describes the naval battles which took place on this restricted sea and mentions the numerous boats which surrounded the Roman vessels. It was, no doubt, on account of the lacustrine position of the city of Tiberias that some of the medals struck in that

The first miraculous Draught of fishes.

town bear on the reverse side a representation of a boat. It is true that on others, struck during the reign of Trajan, this boat is replaced by the figure of the goddess of health in the coils of the serpent, symbolizing Æsculapius, and seated on a mountain from which copious streams of water are issuing, an allusion to the warm springs for which Tiberias was celebrated.

It was from the boat of Simon, later to become a fisher of men, that Jesus brought about the first miraculous draught of fishes, which was a type of the conversions of the future. It was in the same boat, which then symbolized the Church, that Our Lord stilled the tempest and reassured the disciples, who typified redeemed mankind.

Jesus healing the lame and the blind on the Mountain.   J.-J. T.

Jesus healing the lame and the blind
ON THE MOUNTAIN
Saint Matthew — Chap. 15

T accesserunt ad eum turbæ multæ, habentes secum mutos, cæcos, claudos, debiles et alios multos, et projecerunt eos ad pedes ejus, et curavit eos.

ND great multitudes came unto him, having with them *those that were* lame, blind, dumb, maimed, and many others, and cast them down at Jesus' feet; and he healed them :

31. Ita ut turbæ mirarentur, videntes mutos loquentes, claudos ambulantes, cæcos videntes; et magnificabant Deum Israel.

31. Insomuch that the multitude wondered, when they saw the dumb to speak, the maimed to be whole, the lame to walk, and the blind to see : and they glorified the God of Israel.

The healing of the leper
Saint Mark — Chap. 1

venit ad eum leprosus deprecans eum, et genu flexo dixit ei : Si vis, potes me mundare.

And there came a leper to him, beseeching him, and kneeling down to him, and saying unto him, If thou wilt, thou canst make me clean.

41. Jesus autem misertus ejus extendit manum suam, et tangens eum ait illi : Volo; mundare.

42. Et quum dixisset, statim discessit ab eo lepra, et mundatus est.

43. Et comminatus est ei, statimque ejecit illum,

44. Et dicit ei : Vide, nemini dixeris; sed vade, ostende te principi sacerdotum, et offer pro emundatione tua quæ præcepit Moyses in testimonium illis.

41. And Jesus, moved with compassion, put forth *his* hand, and touched him, and saith unto him, I will; be thou clean.

42. And as soon as he had spoken, immediately the leprosy departed from him, and he was cleansed;

43. And he straitly charged him, and forthwith sent him away;

44. And saith unto him, See thou say nothing to any man : but go thy way, shew thyself to the priest, and offer for thy cleansing those things which Moses commanded, for a testimony unto them.

Garden of Dancing Dervishes at Cairo. J.-J. T.

HEALING OF THE LEPERS AT CAPERNAUM

THE HEALING OF THE LEPER

45. At ille egressus cœpit prædicare et diffamare sermonem.

45. But he went out, and began to publish *it* much, and to blaze abroad the matter.

Amongst the Jews there were special laws respecting the lepers, and these sufferers were compelled to take certain precautions to protect their fellow men from coming in contact with them. On all ordinary days of the year the impure, of whom lepers were the chief, had to keep in the middle of the path or road, the undefiled passing by on either side. The rule on feast days was just the reverse, and this difference is easily explained by the desirability of leaving as clear a space as possible for circulation and traffic.

The very soil of the city of Jerusalem was considered sacred, and therefore lepers could not enter it until their recovery had been certified by the Priests. The covered-in space under the gates of the town was, however, given up to them. Here they took shelter from the heat of the sun and from the rain, and were very conveniently placed for receiving alms. No doubt when it was fine, they went outside their refuge, as they do at the present day.

In our engraving, the leper is seen in the middle of an almost deserted road, and is flinging himself in the path of Our Lord, to implore Him to heal him.

We read in the Gospel that Jesus, after He had wrought his cure, charged the leper to go and shew himself to the Priest and fulfil the law. This law required a ceremony curious enough. The man who was cured took two undefiled birds and a bouquet made up of a branch of cedar with one of hyssop, tied together with a band of scarlet wool. One of the birds was sacrificed and the blood received in a vessel containing water. The bunch of cedar and hyssop was then fastened to the other bird and plunged with it into the bloody water, the leper was sprinkled with this water and the bird was set free alive. The man, thus purified, was then free to return to the society of his fellow men and to the privileges of religion.

Garden of Dancing Dervishes at Cairo.

Jesus teaching the multitude. J.-J. T.

Jesus teaching the multitude
Saint Mark – Chap. 2

T egressus est rursus ad mare, omnisque turba veniebat ad eum, et docebat eos.

ND he went forth again by the sea side; and all the multitude resorted unto him, and he taught them.

In the crowd seated at the feet of Jesus and listening to Him, men of many different races are to be seen. There are wealthy citizens of Tiberias, an essentially modern town at that period; there are Jews in the black and white abayeh; Africans, with loose mantles, wearing no sash or belt; women of Samaria and from the shores of the Jordan; and lastly, men from the North; for Tiberias was a halting-place for those who travelled from the North to the South, from Persia to Egypt.

The Calling of Saint Matthew
Saint Matthew — Chap. 9

T quum transiret inde Jesus, vidit hominem sedentem in telonio, Matthæum nomine, et ait illi : Sequere me. Et surgens secutus est eum.

ND as Jesus passed forth from thence, he saw a man, named Matthew, sitting at the receipt of custom : and he saith unto him, Follow me. And he arose, and followed him.

S. MARC. — C. 2

13. Et egressus est rursus ad mare, omnisque turba veniebat ad eum, et docebat eos.

14. Et quum præteriret, vidit Levi Alphæi sedentem ad telonium, et ait illi : Sequere me. Et surgens secutus est eum.

S. MARK. — CH. 2

13. And he went forth again by the seaside; and all the multitude resorted unto him, and he taught them.

14. And as he passed by, he saw Levi the *son* of Alphæus sitting at the receipt of custom, and said unto him, Follow me. And he arose and followed him.

Capernaum, situated on the road from Damascus to the Mediterranean, was a much frequented halting-place, and numerous caravans, with crowds of travellers, passed through it day by day on their

way to Samaria, Judæa, Egypt or, in the other direction, to Persia and the valley of the Euphrates. It was the great emporium of Eastern Galilee, and in it, as well as at other points of this border district, were stationed publicans or custom officers, who collected taxes in the name of the Imperial Treasury. Everywhere in Palestine, at the entrance ports, at the bridges, at the gates of towns, these imposts were exacted, and they weighed very heavily on the people. As a result, the collectors of the taxes were universally hated, and, as is generally the case in matters of this sort, it was the subalterns, who, though less responsible, were more easily accessible, and who came in for most of the odium. Everyone looked upon them as extortioners and tyrants on whom it seemed permissible to heap all manner of maledictions. This was especially the case in the eyes of the Jews, with whom the profession of a publican involved a sort of religious and national apostasy. To take service under Cæsar, as the agent of an odious and oppressive exaction, was tacitly to recognise the domination of the foreigner, not only, as with others, to suffer it. Was not the man who could do this a mere hypocrite to call himself a son of Israel and go up to the Temple to present offerings which were thus defiled? On certain occasions, even Jesus Himself seemed to have adopted this way of looking at the matter, for He did not hesitate to say, when He was speaking of the disciple who neglected to hear the Church : « Let him be unto thee as a heathen man and a publican. »

For all that, however, there were honest men even amongst the publicans, who suffered from, without understanding, the popular prejudice against them. There had been some such amongst the disciples of John the Baptist, and he had not told them to give up their calling, but had merely urged them to pursue it honestly. In spite of this, great must have been the astonishment of the disciples when Jesus called to Him a publican, named Levi bar Alphæus, or Levi, the son of Alphæus, henceforth to be known as Matthew, a name signifying « the gift of God ». He himself must fully have realized the value of that gift, and his heart must have been overflowing with gratitude. It is this feeling we have endeavoured to express.

Saint Matthew.   J.-J. T.

The lost Piece of Silver
Saint Luke – Chap. 15

ut quæ mulier habens drachmas decem, si perdiderit drachmam unam, nonne accendit lucernam et everrit domum et quærit diligenter, donec inveniat ?

9. Et quum invenerit, convocat amicas

ITHER what woman having ten pieces of silver, if she lose one piece, doth not light a candle, and sweep the house, and seek diligently till she find it ?

9. And when she hath found it,

et vicinas, dicens : Congratulamini mihi, quia inveni drachmam, quam perdideram?

she calleth *her* friends and *her* neighbours together, saying, Rejoice with me; for I have found the piece which I had lost.

10. Ita dico vobis, gaudium erit coram angelis Dei super uno peccatore pœnitentiam agente.

The lost Piece of Silver. J. J. T.

10. Likewise, I say unto you, there is joy in the presence of the angels of God over one sinner that repenteth.

Jesus sat at meat with Matthew
Saint Matthew — Chap. 9

T factum est discumbente eo in domo, ecce multi publicani et peccatores venientes discumbebant cum Jesu et discipulis ejus.

11. Et videntes Pharisæi dicebant discipulis ejus : Quare cum publicanis et peccatoribus manducat magister vester?

12. At Jesus audiens ait : Non est opus valentibus medicus, sed male habentibus.

13. Euntes autem discite quid est Misericordiam volo, et non sacrificium.

ND it came to pass, as Jesus sat at meat in the house, behold, many publicans and sinners came and sat down with him and his disciples.

11. And when the Pharisees saw *it*, they said unto his disciples, Why eateth your Master with publicans and sinners?

12. But when Jesus heard *that*, he said unto them, They that be whole need not a physician, but they that are sick.

13. But go ye and learn what *that* meaneth, I will have mercy, and not

Jesus sat at meat with Matthew. J.-J. T.

Non enim veni vocare justos, sed peccatores.

sacrifice: for I am not come to call the righteous, but sinners to repentance.

Christ healing the withered hand
Saint Mark — Chap. 3

T introivit iterum in synagogam, et erat ibi homo habens manum aridam.

2. Et observabant eum, si sabbatis curaret, ut accusarent illum.

ND he entered again into the synagogue; and there was a man there which had a withered hand.

2. And they watched him, whether he would heal him on the sabbath day; that they might accuse him.

CHRIST HEALING THE WITHERED HAND

3. Et ait homini habenti manum aridam : Surge in medium.

4. Et dicit eis : Licet sabbatis bene facere, an male ? animam salvam facere, an perdere ? At illi tacebant.

5. Et circumspiciens eos cum ira, contristatus super cæcitate cordis eorum dicit homini : Extende manum tuam. Et extendit, et restitua est manus illi.

3. And he saith unto the man which had the withered hand, Stand forth.

4. And he saith unto them, Is it lawful to do good on the sabbath days, or to do evil ? to save life, or to kill ? But they held their peace.

5. And when he had looked round about on them with anger, being grieved for the hardness of their hearts, he saith unto the man, Stretch forth thine hand. And he stretched *it* out : and his hand was restored whole as the other.

Christ healing the withered hand.

According to an old tradition related in the Apocryphal Gospel of the Nazarenes, or of the Ebionite Christians, the man with the withered hand was a stone-cutter or mason. Saint Jerome sees in this incident a type of Judaism, in which the hand without strength had become useless and incapable of co-operating in the building of the Temple of God.

We are told in the sacred text that the enemies of Jesus, seeing Him with a sufferer on the Sabbath day, « watched Him, that they might accuse Him » in public if He healed him. Such an idea seems very strange to us, but it was less so in the eyes of Jewish formalists, accustomed as they were to all manner of petty prejudices. The Jewish laws relating to the Sabbath led to positively fantastic discussions between the Rabbis ; indeed, they themselves came to the conclusion that it was impossible to get at the full truth on the subject ; all the more reason was there to give up the idea of an absolute rigidity of observance. Certain amongst the Rabbis held that if the Jewish people could observe exactly two Sabbath days, they would be delivered from all their woes.

The Gospel narrative tells us that, at the time of Our Lord's Ministry, it was lawful, « if a sheep fell into a pit on the Sabbath day,.... to lift it out »: later, however, this concession was withdrawn, and the Rabbis only grudgingly permitted the necessary feeding of animals on the seventh day. It was also forbidden to peel or cook an apple, to kill a flea, a fly or any other insect larger than a certain specified size, or to play on any instrument loud enough to wake a sleeping infant. Yet the sect known as that of the Samaritans did not consider all these rules quite severe enough. To them, it was against the law of the Sabbath to light a fire, or to move from one's place for any reason, except to go to prayer, or to occupy oneself in any way except by reading the Bible. They actually called the Sabbath day their bride, and prided themselves on being its exclusive possessors, and in shutting out from its enjoyment all the peoples of the world.

The Enemy sowing Tares
Saint Matthew — Chap. 13

 LIAM parabolam proposuit illis, dicens : Simile factum est regnum cœlorum homini, qui seminavit bonum semen in agro suo.

 NOTHER parable put he forth unto them, saying, The kingdom of heaven is likened unto a man which sowed good seed in his field :

25. Quum autem dormirent homines, venit inimicus ejus, et superseminavit zizania in medio tritici, et abiit.

26. Quum autem crevisset herba et fructum fecisset, tunc apparuerunt et zizania.

27. Accedentes autem servi patrisfamilias dixerunt ei : Domine, nonne bonum semen seminasti in agro tuo ? unde ergo habet zizania ?

25. But while men slept, his enemy came and sowed tares among the wheat, and went his way.

26. But when the blade was sprung up, and brought forth fruit, then appeared the tares also.

27. So the servants of the householder came and said unto him, Sir, didst not thou sow good seed in thy field ? from whence then hath it tares ?

A street in Jerusalem. J.~J T.

THE ENEMY SOWING TARES

28. Et ait illis : Inimicus homo hoc fecit. Servi autem dixerunt ei : Vis, imus et colligimus ea?

29. Et ait : Non, ne forte colligentes zizania eradicetis simul cum eis et triticum.

30. Sinite utraque crescere usque ad messem, et in tempore messis dicam messoribus : Colligite primum zizania et alligate ea in fasciculos ad comburendum, triticum autem congregate in horreum meum.

28. He said unto them, An enemy hath done this. The servants said unto him, Wilt thou then that we go and gather them up?

29. But he said, Nay; lest while ye gather up the tares, ye root up also the wheat with them.

30. Let both grow together until the harvest : and in the time of harvest I will say to the reapers, Gather ye together first the tares, and bind them in bundles to burn them : but gather the wheat into my barn.

The Enemy Sowing Tares. J.-J. T.

The landscape we represent in our engraving is a corner of the valley of Hinnom, situated on the south of Jerusalem. This valley was looked upon with a kind of terror on account of the horrors which it had witnessed.

It was, in fact, near here, and no doubt, not far from the rocks shutting in the valley, that at one time rose up a temple sacred to Moloch, where human victims were sacrificed. The image of the god, who was seated on a throne, was of bronze, and was made in the form of a man, with the head of a bull,

wearing a royal diadem. According to some accounts there was a fiery furnace in the interior of the statue, and at the time of sacrifice, children were placed in the hands of the monster, and then, by some mechanical contrivance, hoisted into his mouth, from which they were drawn into, and consumed by, the fire below. The place under notice was called Tophet, a word meaning « drums », because, it is said, those instruments of music were beaten to drown the sobs and cries of the children sacrificed to the god.

The Pharisees and the Herodians
Saint Mark — Chap. 3

XEUNTES autem Pharisæi statim cum Herodianis consilium faciebant adversus eum, quomodo eum perderent.   SANCT. MARC. — C. 3.

ND the Pharisees went forth, and straightway took counsel with the Herodians against him, how they might destroy him.   SAINT MARK. — CH. 3.

The spot represented in our engraving is near a synagogue, and trees had been planted there to afford shelter from the sun to the doctors who frequented it to talk together. The trees chosen were cypresses, pines and cedars, all of a more or less sombre aspect, harmonising well with and accentuating the secluded character of this place sacred to meditation. Seats were contrived in the stone walls, so that the doctors could sit at their ease.

EXPLANATORY NOTES

(1) Page 82 : "That which is born of the flesh is flesh; and that which is born of the Spirit is spirit."

That is to say: Through his natural birth man's nature is earthly, animal, sinful; by baptismal regeneration he receives a higher life, he is purified and sanctified, he becomes the child of God. (Cornel. a Lap., Menochius, etc.)

(2) Page 101 : "Preaching the Gospel of the Kingdom."

The Good News that the Kingdom of Heaven was at hand. (Menochius.)

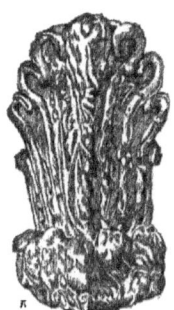

Jewish Ornament. J.-J. T.

LIST OF ILLUSTRATIONS

OF THE FIRST VOLUME

FULL PAGE ILLUSTRATIONS

	Page
The Adoration of the Magi (Frontispiece)	
Jesus shewing Himself through the lattice (Title Page)	
The *Magnificat*	10
Saint Joseph seeks a lodging at Bethlehem	16
The Massacre of the Innocents	30
The Childhood of Saint John the Baptist	32
Jesus found	42
The Winnower	58
The Baptism of Jesus	62
Calling of Saint Andrew and Saint John	69
"All the City was gathered together at the door"	98
Healing of the Lepers at Capernaum	110

ILLUSTRATIONS IN THE TEXT

Zacharias and Elizabeth	1
The Vision of Zacharias	4
The Testing of the Suitors of the Virgin	5
The Betrothal of the Holy Virgin and Saint Joseph	6
The Annunciation	8
The Holy Virgin as a girl	8
The Visitation	9
The Anxiety of Saint Joseph	12
Saint Joseph	13
The Vision of Saint Joseph	16
The Nativity of Our Lord and Saviour Jesus Christ	17
Gloria in excelsis Deo	20
The Adoration of the Shepherds	21
The Aged Simeon	23
The Presentation of Jesus in the Temple	24
Saint Anna	25
The Magi on their way to Bethlehem	28

LIST OF ILLUSTRATIONS

	Page
Interview of the Magi with Herod	28
The Flight into Egypt	32
The Sojourn in Egypt	33
The Return from Egypt	36
Jesus and His Mother at the Fountain	37
Jesus Lost	40
Jesus sitting in the midst of the Doctors	41
The Youth of Jesus	44
Union in Prayer	55
The Voice in the Desert	56
"The Ax laid unto the root of the Tree"	57
Saint John the Baptist and the Pharisees	60
Saint John the Baptist sees Jesus from afar	61
Jesus taken up into an high Mountain	63
Jesus tempted in the Wilderness	64
Jesus set upon a pinnacle of the Temple	65
Saint John	67
Jesus ministered to by Angels	68
The Calling of Saint Peter and Saint Andrew	69
Saint Andrew	70
The Calling of Saint James and Saint John	72
Nathanael under the fig-tree	73
Saint Bartholomew	74
The Betrothed of Cana of Galilee	76
The Marriage in Cana	77
Jesus goes up to Jerusalem	80
Interview between Jesus and Nicodemus	81
Nicodemus	82
The Disciples of Jesus baptizing	84
The Man with an infirmity of thirty and eight years	85
The Piscina Probatica	88
The Woman of Samaria at the Well	89
Saint Philip	90
Jesus in the Synagogue	92
The Brow of the Hill near Nazareth	93
The Hidden Treasure	94
The Man at the Plough	95
The Man with an unclean Spirit in the Synagogue	96
Healing of Simon's wife's mother	97
Saint Simon	98
The Man who laid up Treasure	99
Jesus went out into a desert place	100
Jesus teaching in the Synagogue	101
The vine dresser and the fig-tree	102
Saint Paul	103
The healing of the Ruler's son	104
Jesus preaching in a ship	105
Saint James the Greater	107

LIST OF ILLUSTRATIONS

	Page
The first miraculous Draught of Fishes	108
Jesus healing the lame and the blind on the Mountain	109
Jesus teaching the multitude	112
The Calling of Saint Matthew	113
Saint Matthew	114
The Lost Piece of Silver	115
Jesus sat at meat with Matthew	116
Christ healing the withered hand	117
The enemy sowing tares	119
The Pharisees and the Herodians	120

SUPPLEMENTARY ILLUSTRATIONS,
FAC-SIMILE WOOD ENGRAVINGS AFTER DRAWINGS

Lamps in the Mosque of El-Aksa	XIII
Fountain of the Virgin at Aïn-Karim	3
Plan of the House at Nazareth	7
View of Nazareth	15
Plan of the Grotto of the Nativity at Bethlehem	18
A Typical Jewish Armenian	19
The Citadel of Cairo. View taken from Mount Mokatam	35
Mount Mokatam. View taken from the Citadel of Cairo	38
Cloisters of the Mehemet Ali Mosque	40
Haram : Mosque of Es-Sakhra, called the Mosque of Omar, Jerusalem	42
Typical Jews	43
Bas-relief from the El-Aksa Mosque	45
Jewish Ornament	49
Ossuary	54
Mountains near Jericho	59
The Lake of Gennesaret, near the site of Bethsaida	71
In Old Cairo	75
Phœnician Capital	75
In Old Cairo	78
An Armenian	79
Ornament in gilded metal from the Es-Sakhra mosque	79
In the Island of Rhoda, Old Cairo	83
Phœnician Capital	83
A typical woman of Jerusalem	86
A Synagogue in Jerusalem	91
Two Columns, Jerusalem	97
A Corner in the Valley of Hinnom	106
Judaic Ornament	108
Garden of Dancing Dervishes at Cairo	110
Garden of Dancing Dervishes at Cairo	111
A Street in Jerusalem	118

GENERAL INDEX OF THE CONTENTS

OF THE FIRST VOLUME

THE HOLY CHILDHOOD

	Page
DEDICATION	III
INTRODUCTION	IX
Vision of Zacharias	1
The Testing of the Suitors of the Virgin	5
Betrothal of the Holy Virgin and Saint Joseph	6
The Annunciation	7
The Visitation	9
The Magnificat	10
The Anxiety of Saint Joseph	12
The Vision of Saint Joseph	14
Saint Joseph seeks a lodging at Bethlehem	16
The Nativity of Our Lord and Saviour Jesus Christ	17
"Gloria in excelsis Deo"	19
The Adoration of the Shepherds	21
Presentation of Jesus in the Temple	22
The Magi on their journey	26
The Wise Men and Herod	27
The Adoration of the Magi	29
The Massacre of the Innocents	30
The Childhood of St. John the Baptist	31
The Flight into Egypt	32
The Sojourn in Egypt	33
The Return from Egypt	34
Jesus and His Mother at the Fountain	36
Jesus lost	37
Jesus amidst the doctors	39
Jesus found	41
The Youth of Jesus	43
EXPLANATORY NOTES	46

THE MINISTRY

INTRODUCTION	51
Union in Prayer	55

GENERAL INDEX OF THE CONTENTS OF THE FIRST VOLUME

	Page
The Voice in the Desert	56
"The Ax laid unto the root of the tree"	57
"He who fans his wheat"	58
Saint John the Baptist and the Pharisees	59
Saint John the Baptist sees Jesus from afar	61
The Baptism of Jesus	62
Jesus taken up into an high mountain	63
Jesus tempted in the wilderness	64
Jesus set upon a pinnacle of the Temple	66
Jesus ministered to by Angels	68
The Calling of Saint Andrew and Saint John	69
The Calling of Saint Peter and Saint Andrew	71
The Calling of Saint James and Saint John	72
Nathanael under the fig-tree	73
The Betrothed of Cana of Galilee	76
The Marriage in Cana	76
Jesus goes up to Jerusalem	80
Interview between Jesus and Nicodemus	81
The Disciples of Jesus baptizing	84
The Man with an infirmity of thirty-and-eight years	85
The Piscina Probatica or Pool of Bethesda	87
The Woman of Samaria at the well	89
Jesus in the Synagogue	91
The brow of the hill near Nazareth	93
The Hidden Treasure	94
The Man at the Plough	94
The Man with an unclean Spirit in the Synagogue	95
The Healing of Simon's wife's mother	97
"All the city was gathered together"	98
The man who laid up Treasure	99
Jesus went out into a desert place	100
Jesus teaching in the Synagogue	101
The Vine dresser and the fig-tree	102
The healing of the Ruler's son	103
Jesus preaching in a ship	105
The first miraculous Draught of Fishes	106
Jesus healing the lame and the blind on the Mountain	109
The healing of the Leper	110
Jesus teaching the multitude	112
The Calling of Saint Matthew	113
The lost piece of Silver	114
Jesus sat at meat with Matthew	115
Christ healing the withered hand	116
The enemy sowing tares	118
The Pharisees and the Herodians	120

www.ingramcontent.com/pod-product-compliance
Lightning Source LLC
Chambersburg PA
CBHW022118160426
43197CB00009B/1080